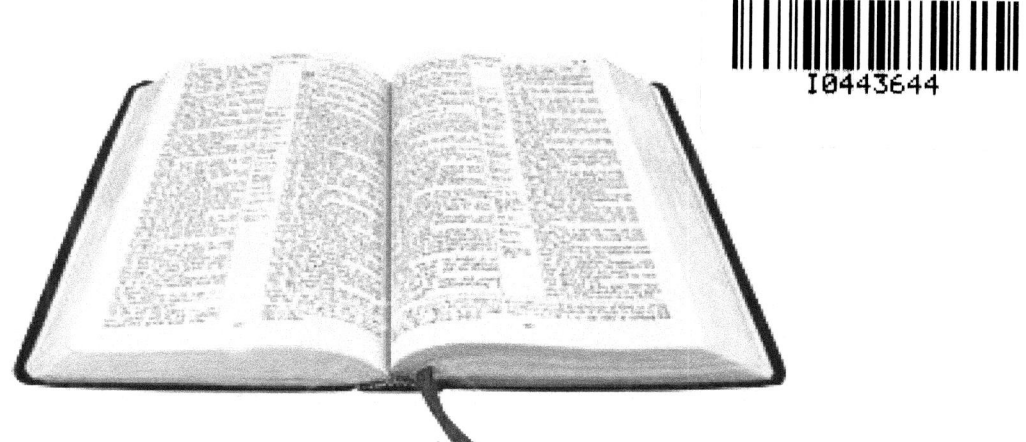

Bible Verses from A-Z Book 1

By Lybid D. Page

ABCDEF
GHIJKL
MNOPQ
RSTUV
WXYZ

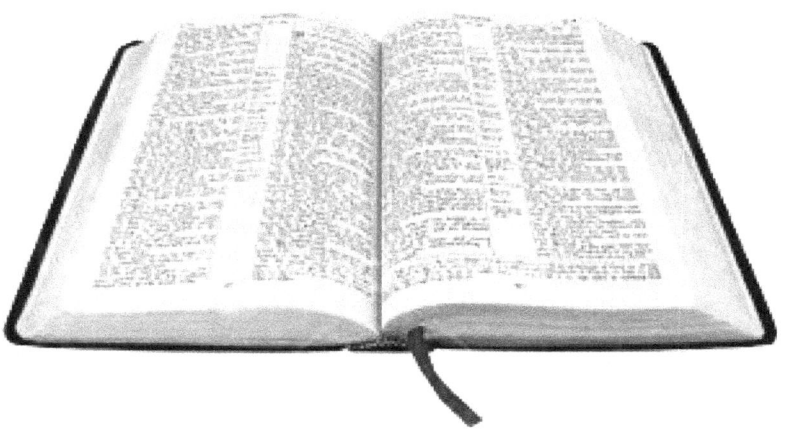

Bible Verses from A-Z Book 1

By Lybid D. Page

ABCDEF
GHIJKL
MNOPQ
RSTUV
WXYZ

Copyright © 2022 Lybid D. Page

All rights reserved
All Scriptures are from
the King James Version of the Bible

KDP ISBN: 9798521453870

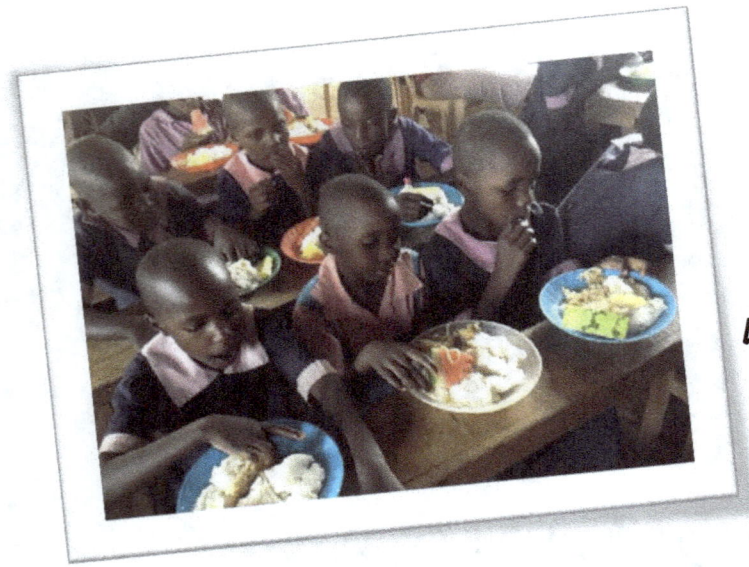

The proceeds from this book will be used to help support the

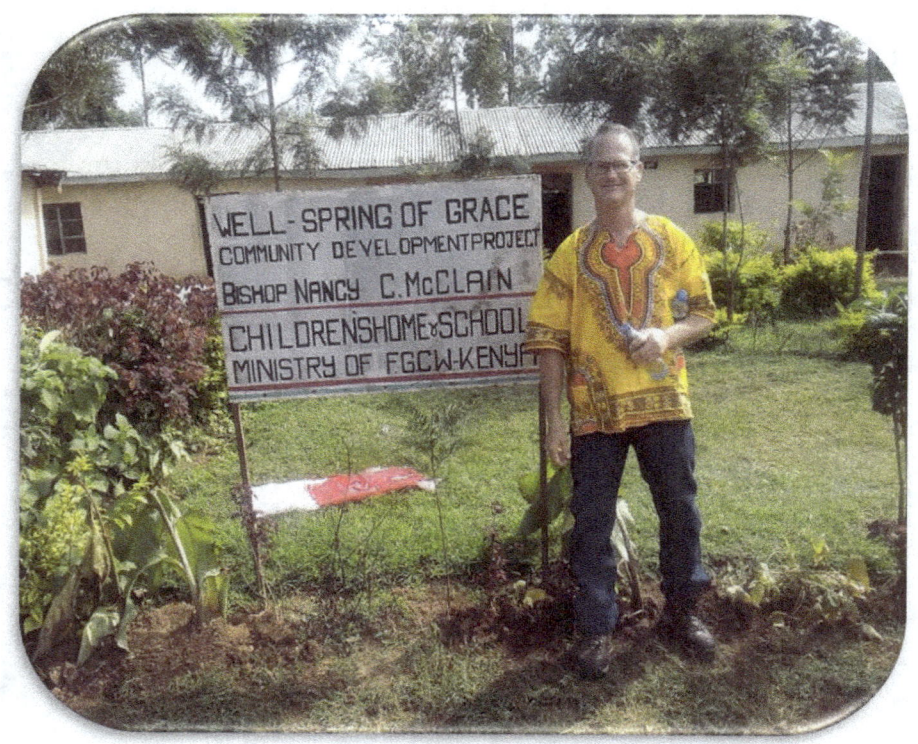

And the King shall answer and say unto them, Verily I say unto you, Inasmuch as ye have done it unto one of the least of these my brethren, ye have done it unto Me.

(Matthew 25:40 KJV)

This book combines scripture verses from A to Z with created illustrations by the author. Lybid is currently recovering from a stroke experienced in June of 2018. One of the ways that have helped her on her journey to healing is by digging into the Word of God on a daily basis. This book encourages you to memorize scriptures no matter what challenges you may be facing in life.

A Receiving from God is simple - **ASK**. Sometimes we don't get an answer because we never asked the question.

ASK, and it shall be given you; seek, and ye shall find; knock, and it shall be opened unto you:

(Matthew 7:7 KJV)

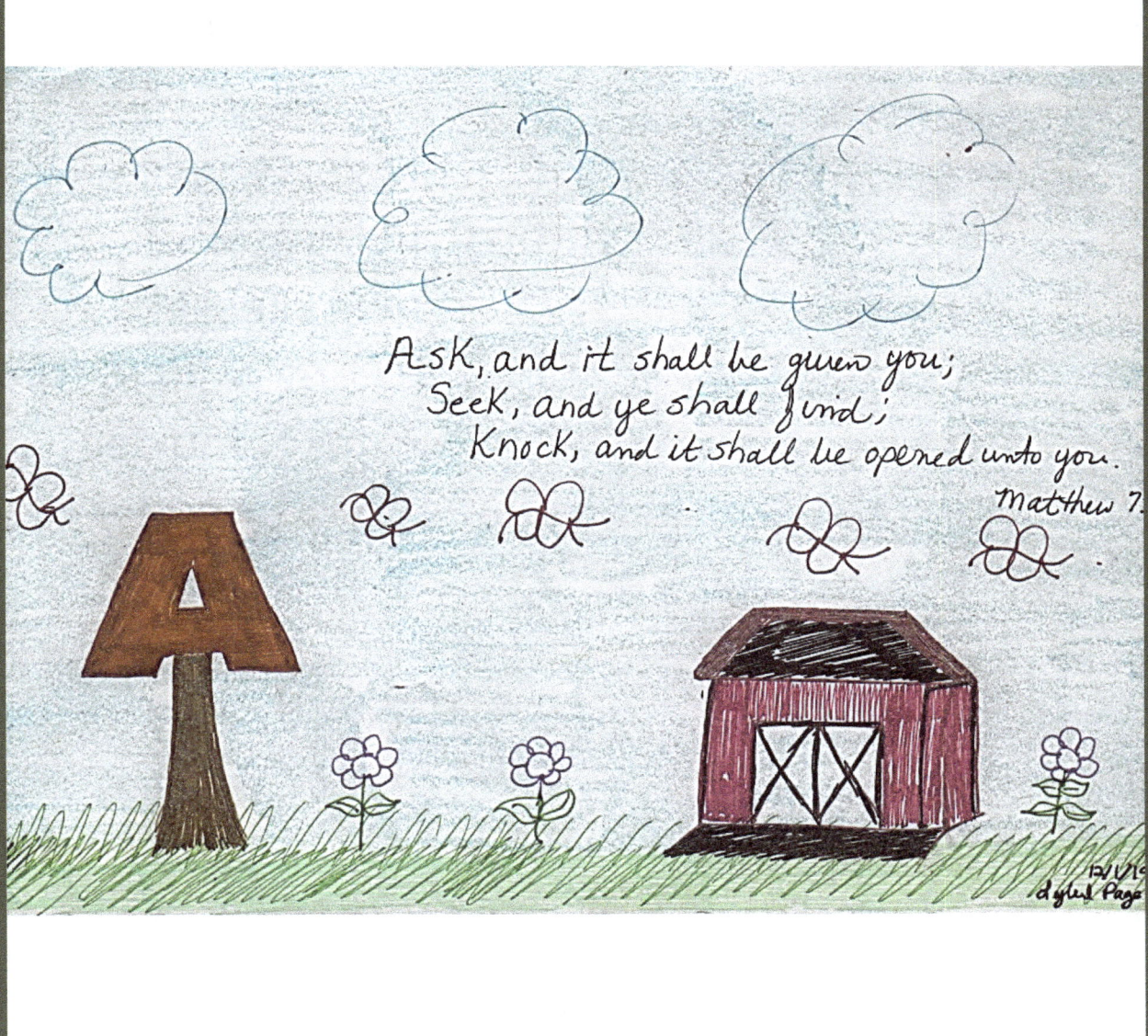

B Do you want a blessed life? Obey the Word of God.

This verse gives us instructions on how to live blessed.

1. Do not walk in the counsel (advise) of the ungodly
2. Do not stand in the way of sinners.
3. Do not sit in the seat of the scornful.

Blessed is the man that walketh
not in the counsel of the ungodly,
nor standeth in the way of sinners,
nor sitteth in the seat of the scornful.

(Psalms 1:1 KJV)

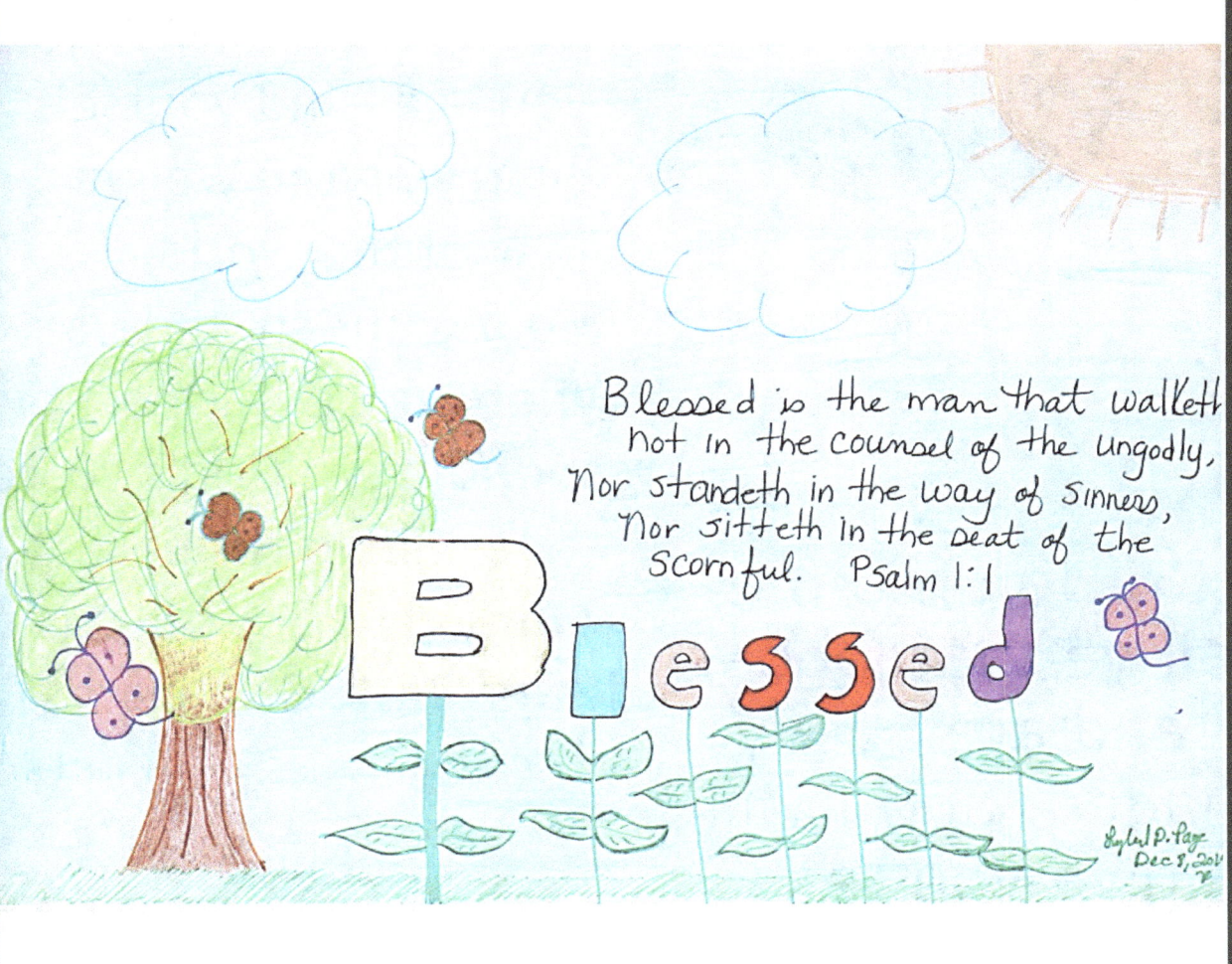

Are you a hard worker? Do you ever find yourself carrying the weight of the world upon your shoulders? When we do our part by responding to God's Word, He will do His part.

Our Part: Go to Jesus
Jesus' Part: Give us rest.

Come unto me, all ye that labour and are heavy laden, and I will give you rest.

(Matthew 11:28 KJV)

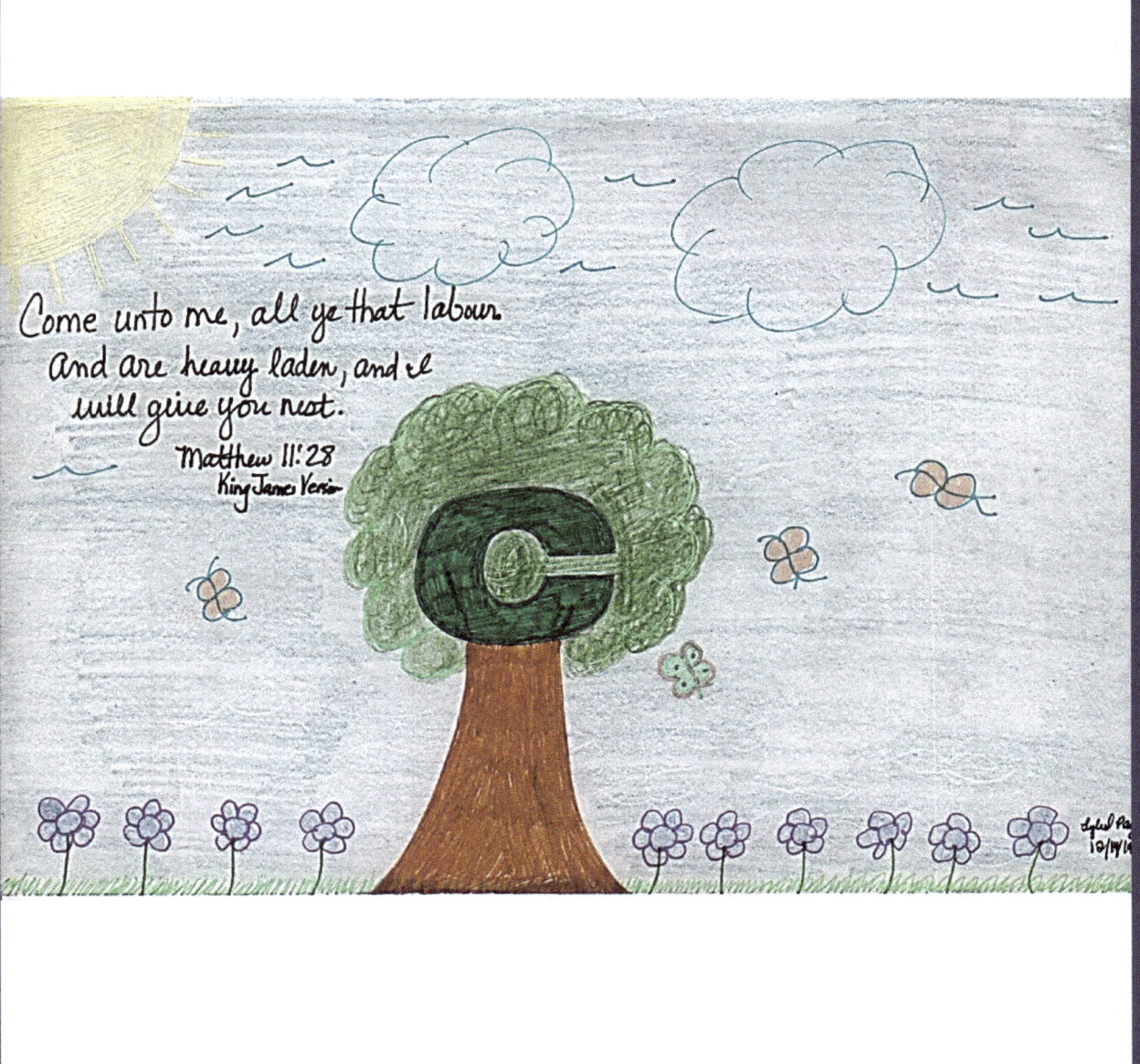

Delight thyself also in the Lord; and He shall give thee the desires of thine heart.

(Psalms 37:4 KJV)

Have you ever wanted a something little extra? Have you ever wanted to do something extra special for yourself? Do you know that God wants to do more than just meet your needs. He wants you to enjoy life. Jesus said, "I've come that you might have life and that more abundantly" (John 10:10).
To experience abundant life is simple.

Our Part: Delight ourselves in the Lord
God's Part: He will give us the desires of our heart

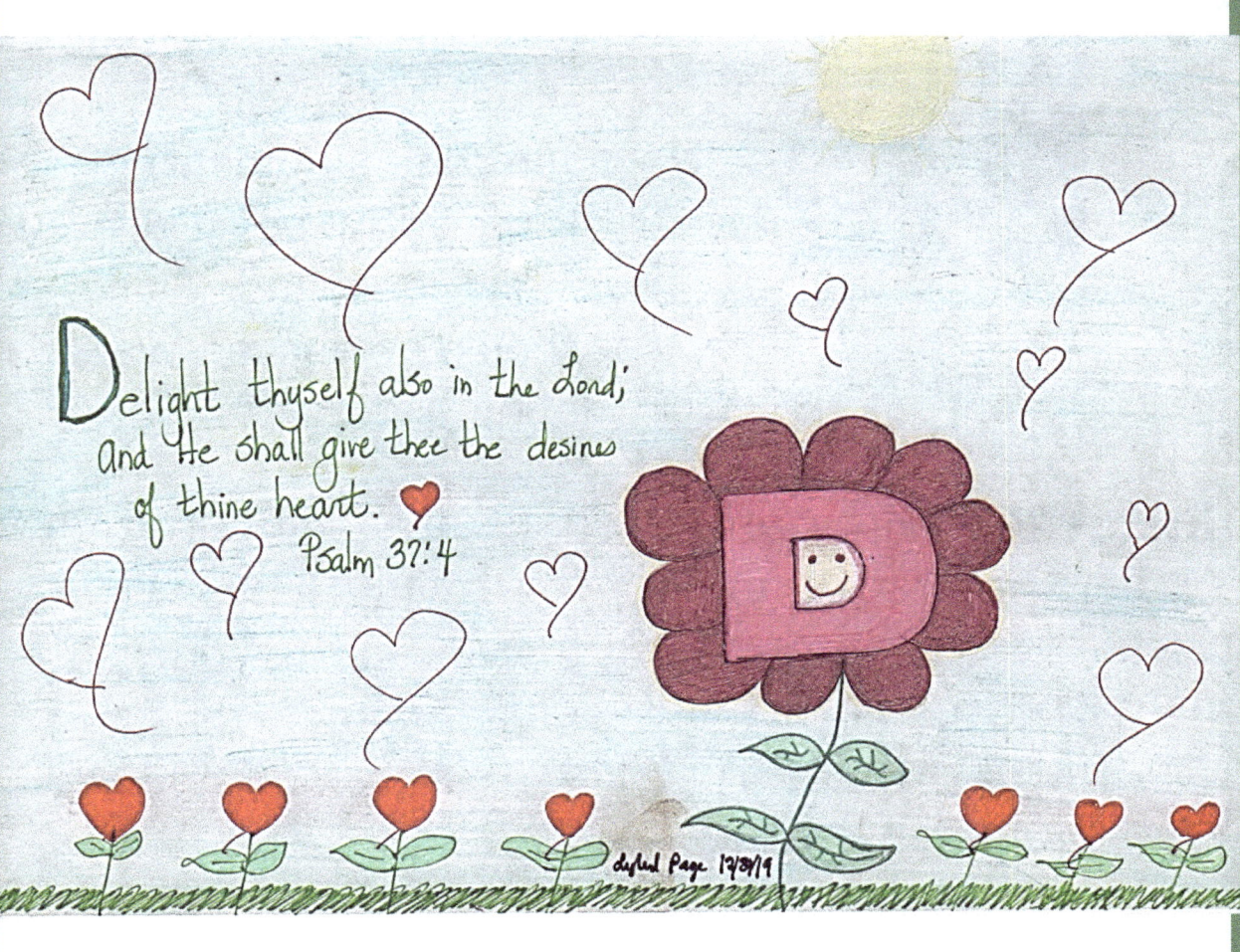

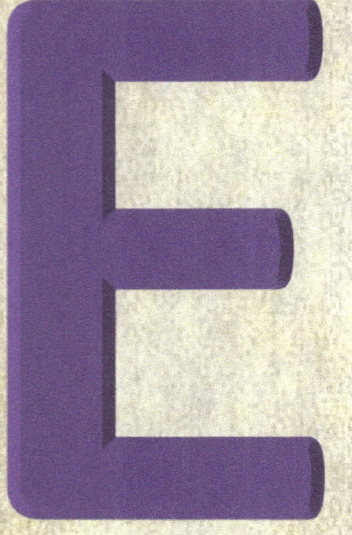

As we read throughout the Bible, we will find that there are more things that God commands us to do than what is found in the Ten commandments in Exodus. This verse gives us a few commands that should be obeyed every day of our lives.

Enter into His gates with thanksgiving, and into His courts with praise: be thankful unto Him, and bless His name.

(Psalms 100:4 KJV)

1. Enter into His gates with Thanksgiving
2. Enter His courts with praise be thankful
3. Bless God's Name

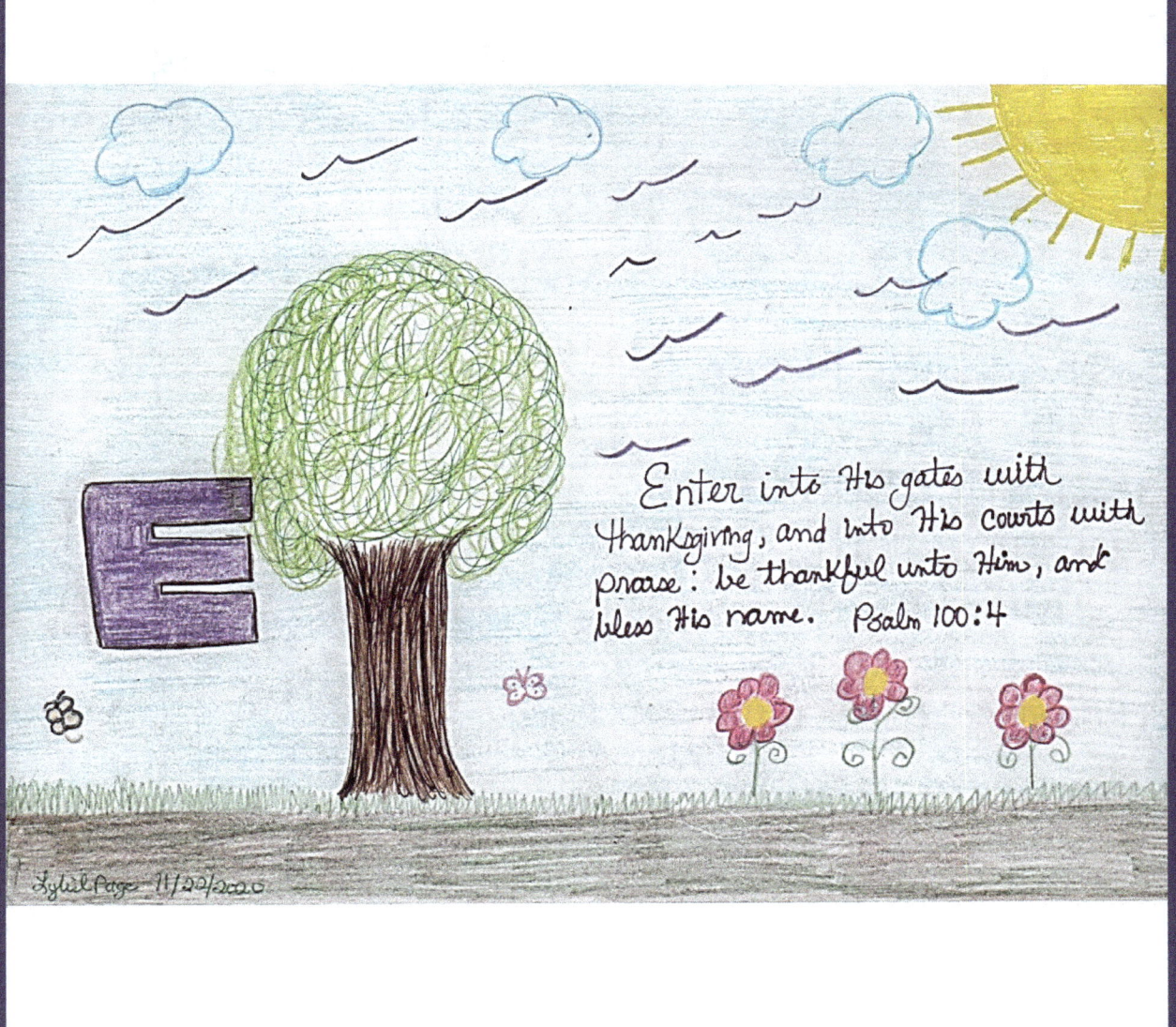

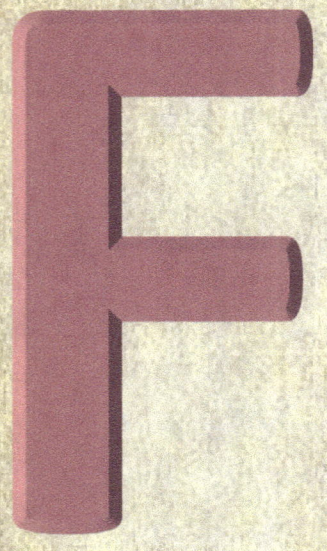

Why should we give God praise? Regardless to what we are going through and regardless to what has happened in our lives we need to understand three things.

1. God is good.
2. His mercy is everlasting.
3. His truth endures to all generations.

For the LORD is good; His mercy is everlasting; and His truth endureth to all generations.

(Psalms 100:5 KJV)

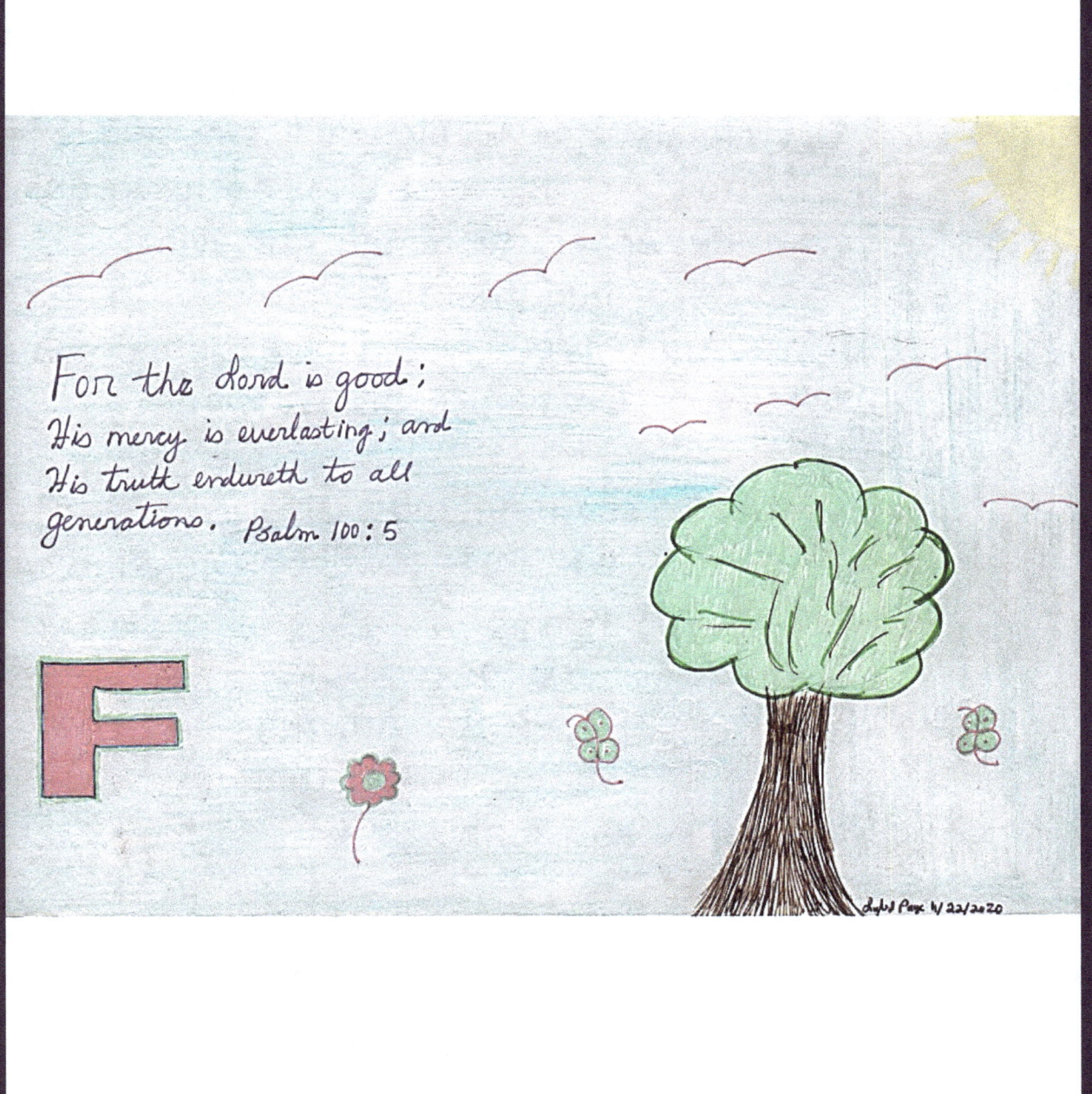

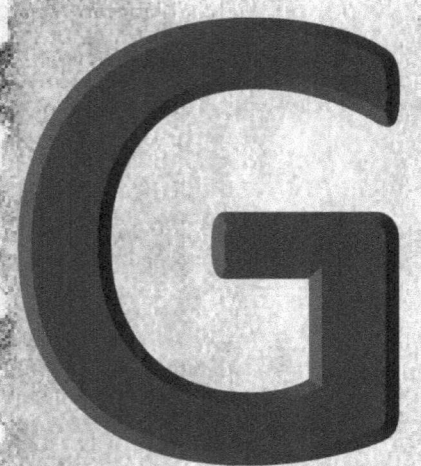
Giving spans every aspect of our lives. When asked to give most people immediately think of money, but it is far more than that. Giving will involve our time, our effort, our energy and our focus. How would you like people to give to you? This verse gives us the results or better yet, the benefits of giving. Remember the Golden rule – "Do unto others as you would have them do unto you." Obedience has a reward.

- **The Command** – Give
- **The Result** – It will be given unto you
- **How** –
    - Good measure
    - Pressed down
    - Shaken together
    - Running over

Give, and it shall be given unto you; good measure, pressed down, and shaken together, and running over, shall men give into your bosom. For with the same measure that ye mete withal it shall be measured to you again.

(Luke 6:38 KJV)

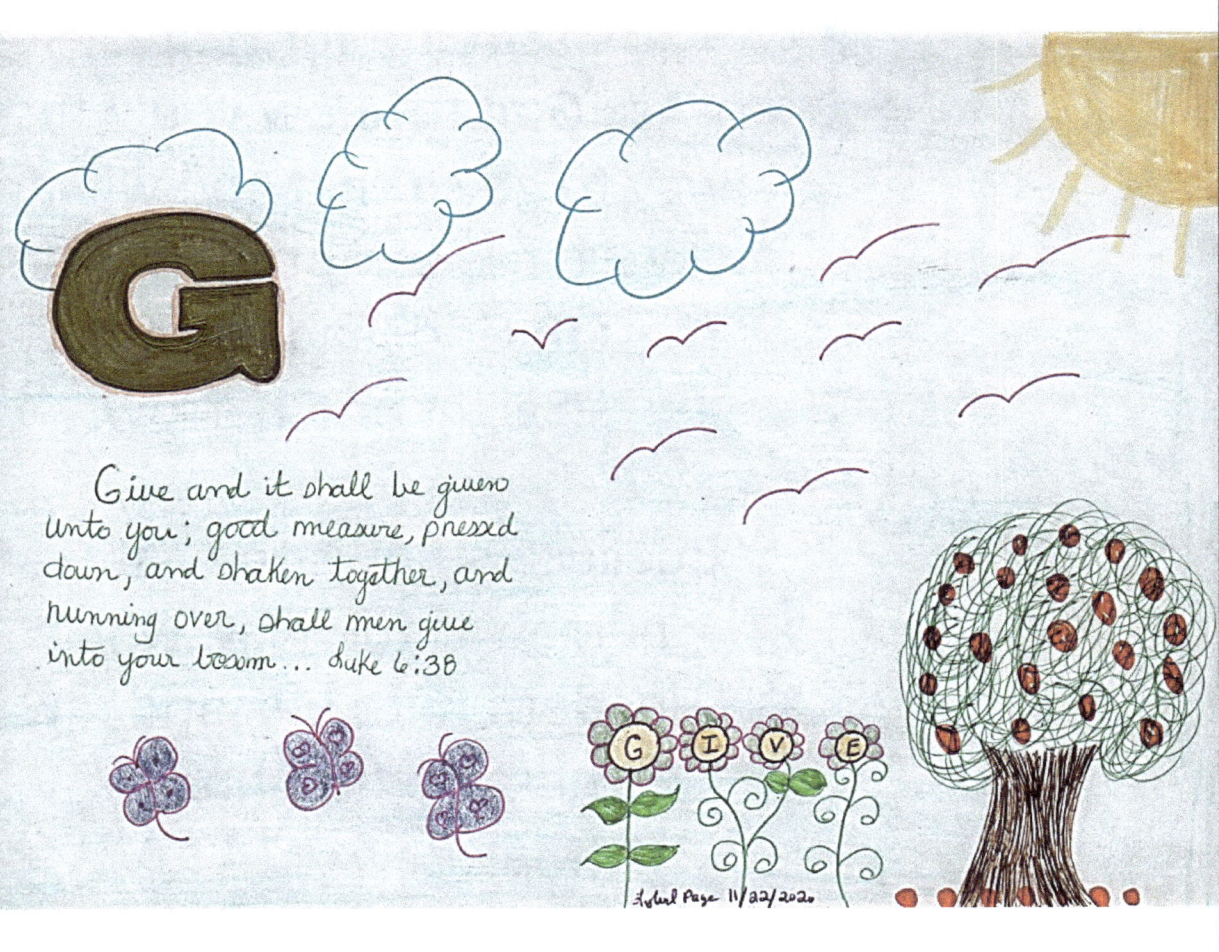

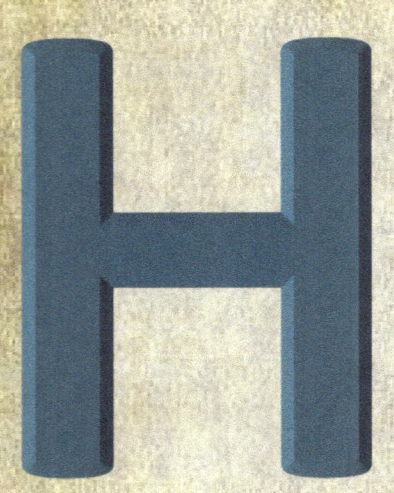

Many new Believers ask, "How can I live without sinning?" The answer is... ask God for Help. Ask God to show you which way to go so that you will not walk into temptation. The path God leads us on is straight and narrow.

"Because strait is the gate, and narrow is the way, which leadeth unto life, and few there be that find it." (Matthew 7:14 KJV)

Hold up my goings in thy paths, that my footsteps slip not.

(Psalms 17:5 KJV)

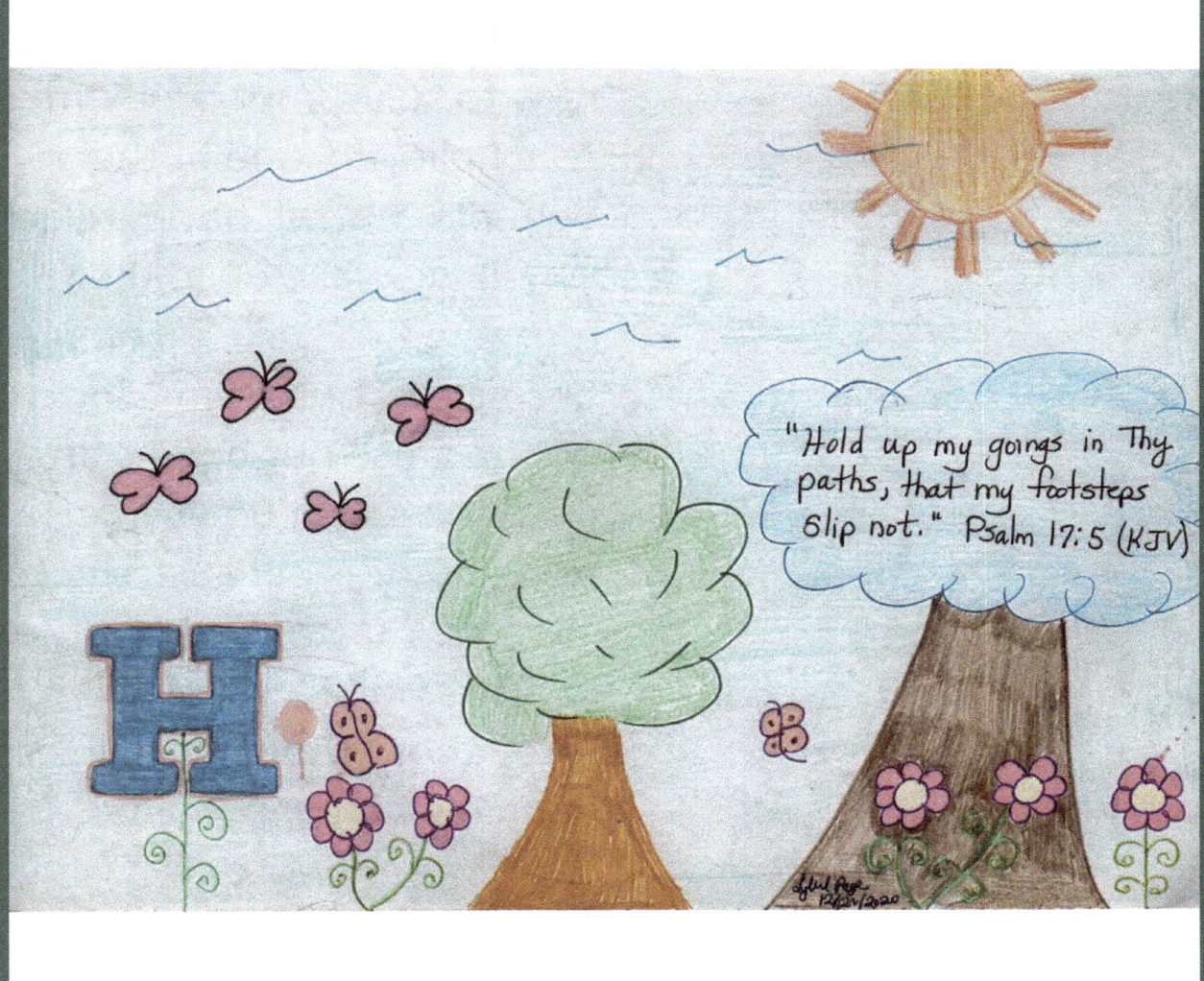

Have you ever been so tired that you laid down, but you couldn't sleep? Do you wake up worried and tired because you were trying to figure out how to solve your problem? As a believer, one of the benefits that we have is sleep. When we wake up in the morning, we wake up not because of our alarm clocks, not because our bodies are used to waking up at a certain time, but it is because the Lord sustained us throughout the night. If God can sustain you throughout the night, He can handle whatever problems comes your way.

I laid me down and slept;
I awaked;
for the Lord sustained me.

(Psalms 3:5 KJV)

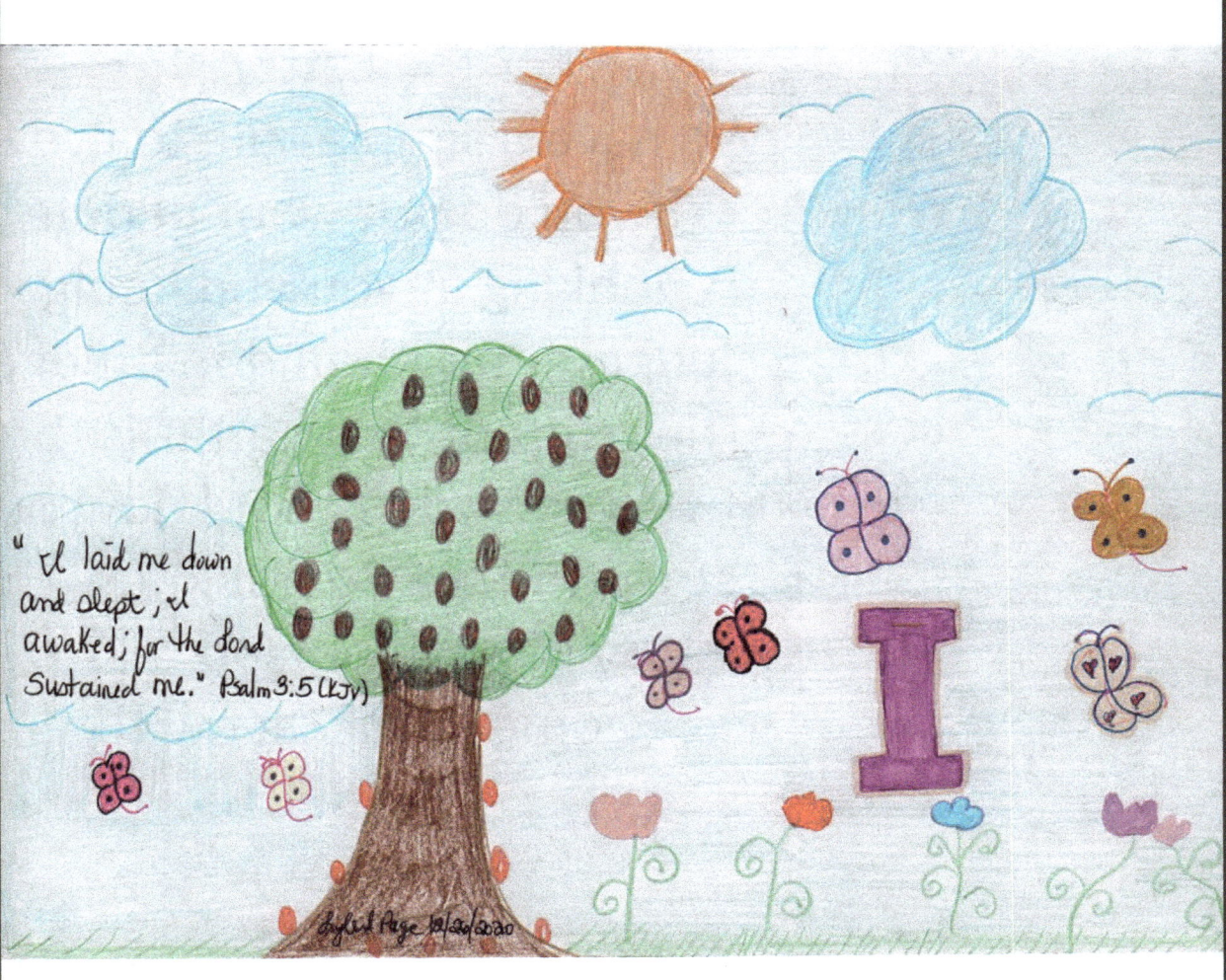

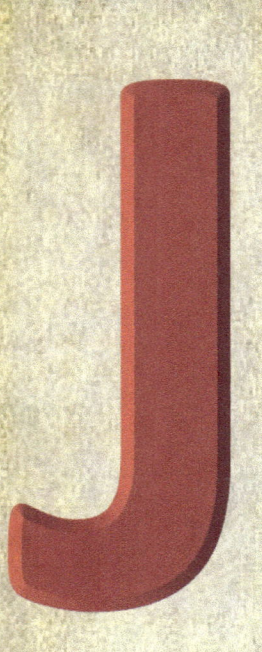

For the Letter "J",
We have a simple rule to live by. If you do not want people looking at you and being judgmental- then don't judge. The truth of the matter is this - everybody does not know our story and we do not know the story of each person that we come in contact with.

Judge not,
that ye be not judged.

(Matthew 7:1 KJV)

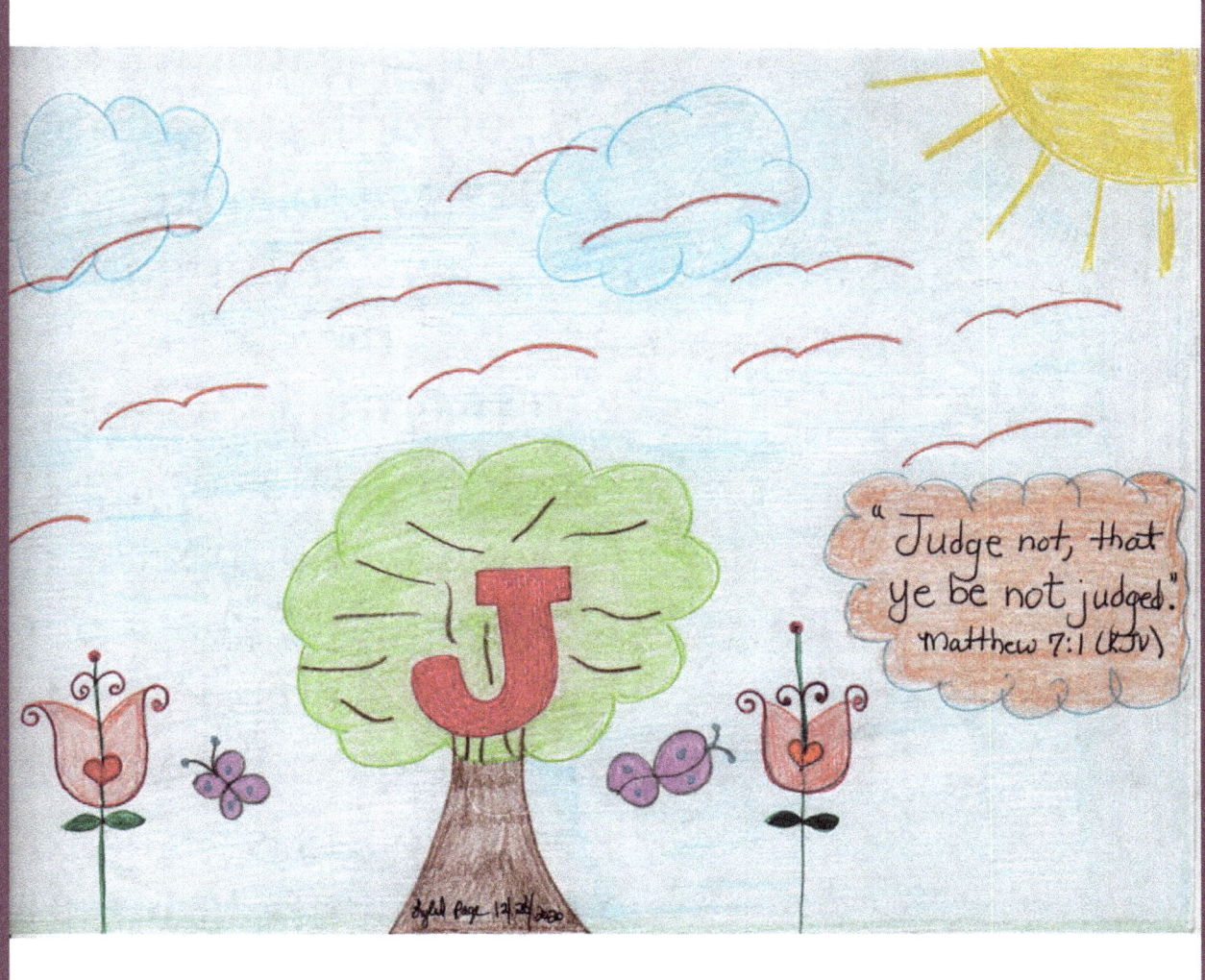

It is important for us to keep our hearts with all diligence.
This means that we have to put forth some effort - we have to make sure that we pay attention to the details.
It tells us in this verse that the issues of life are within our hearts.
We need to guard our hearts because when we least expect it - what in our hearts is going to come out of our mouth.

Keep thy heart with all diligence; for out of it are the issues of life.

(Proverbs 4:23 KJV)

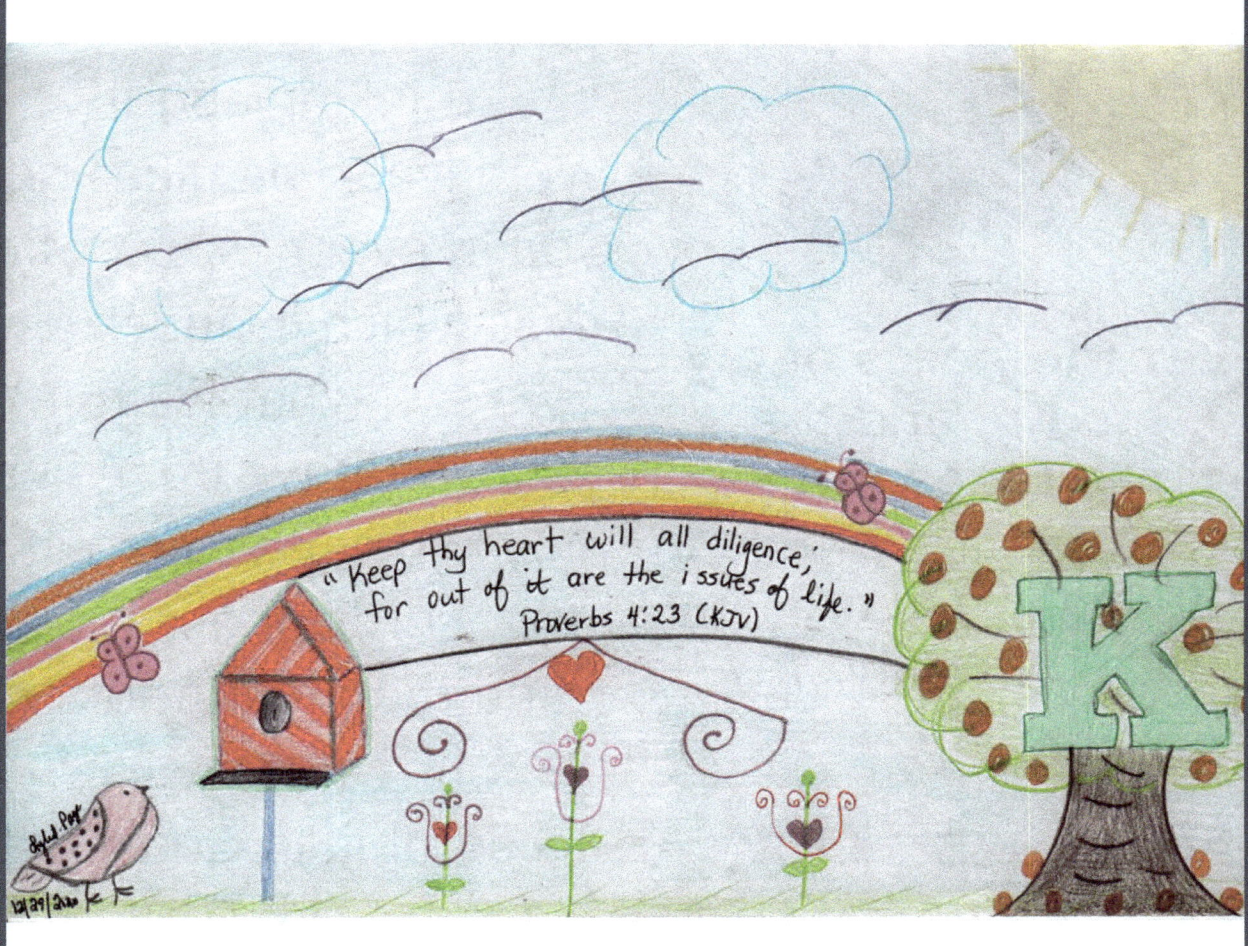

Let the words of my mouth, and the meditation of my heart, be acceptable in Thy sight, O Lord, my Strength, and my Redeemer.

(Psalms 19:14 KJV)

Do you realize that God hears what you say and knows what you are thinking about?
We have to be pleasing to God in every aspect of our lives which includes what we say, what we think, and what we do. As we pray, we need to pray that the words of our mouth and the meditations of our hearts will be acceptable in God's sight. Why?
Because God is our strength and God is our Redeemer.

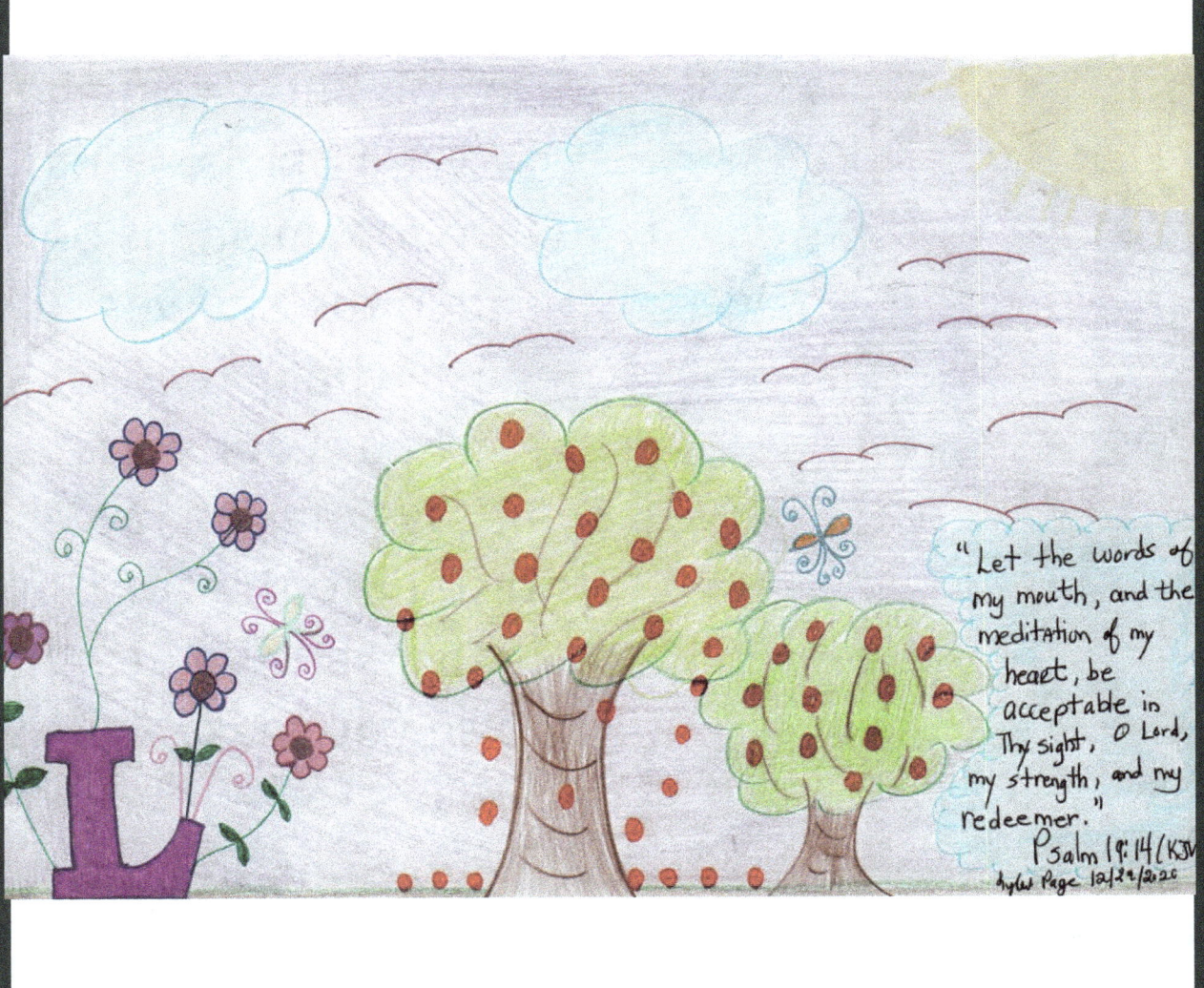

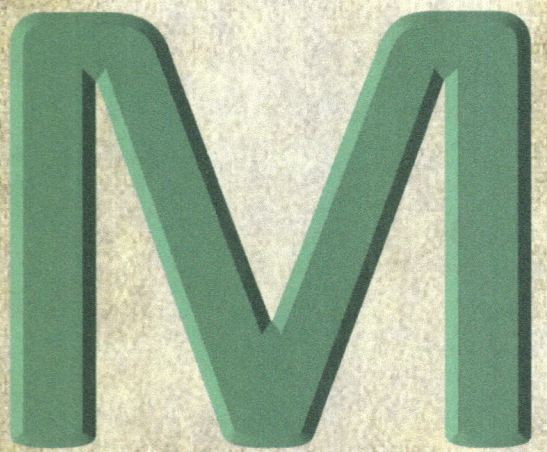

Do you have a singing voice? Maybe your voice for singing is only used in the shower. But guess what God wants to hear your voice. It says make a joyful noise unto the Lord. So that means whatever noise you make - God wants to hear your voice of praise.

Make a joyful noise unto the LORD, all ye lands.

(Psalms 100:1 KJV)

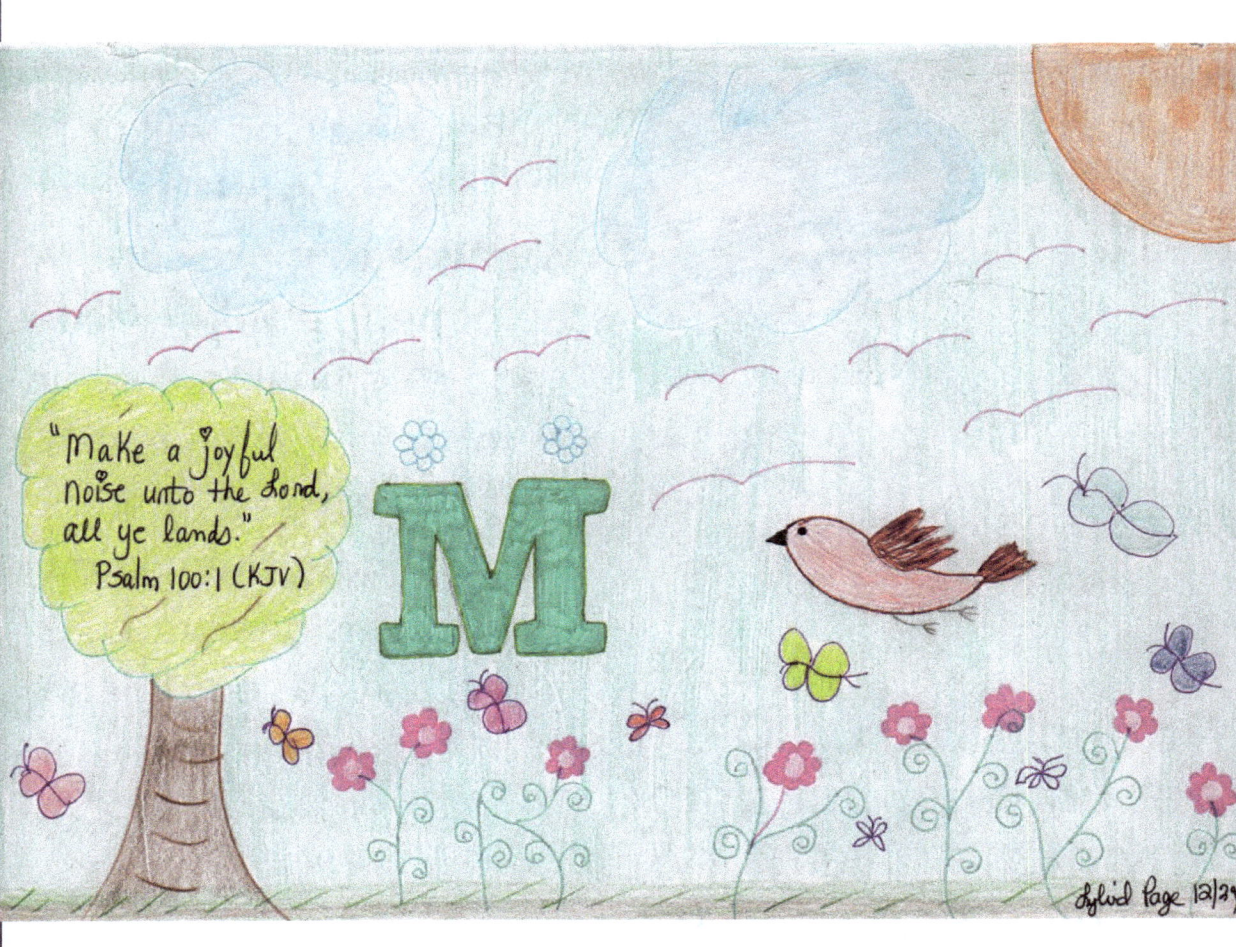

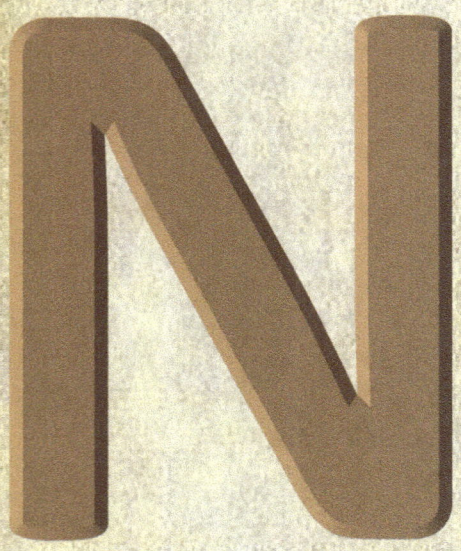

One thing God will not share with us is His Glory. We need to make sure we point people God. When people compliment us on a job well done, we can graciously say "thank you", and let them know that God is one who has gifted us with our talents and abilities.

Not unto us, O LORD, not unto us, but unto Thy name give glory, for Thy mercy, and for Thy truth's sake.

(Psalms 115:1 KJV)

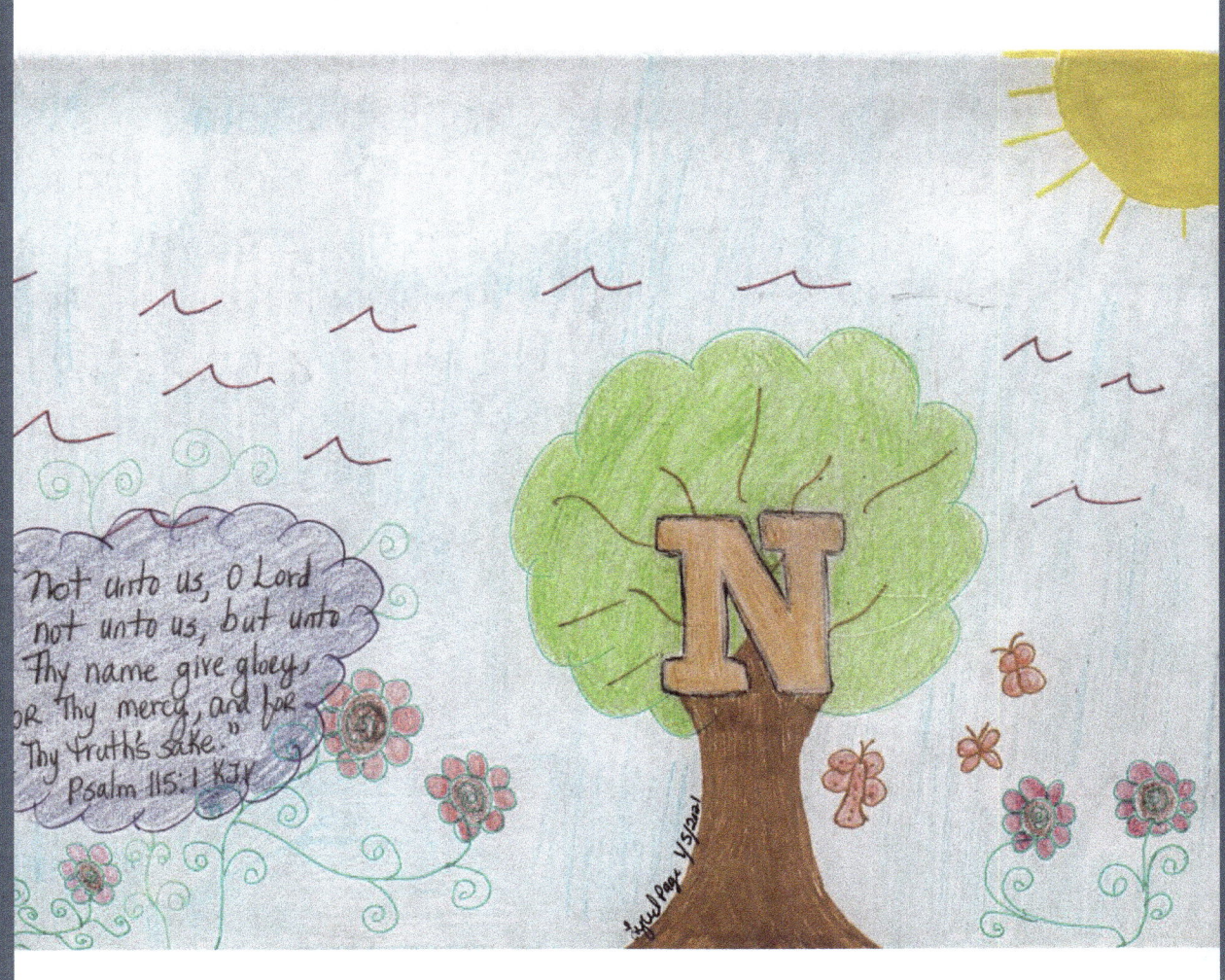

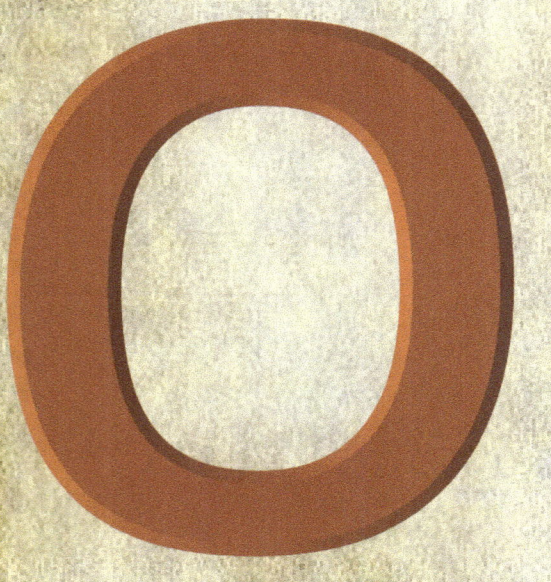

One sure way to deal with depression or feelings of overwhelming sadness is to begin to give thanks unto the Lord. Even if what you are going through is not good, God is. You have a reason to give thanks unto the Lord regardless and in spite of what is happening in your life right now. This verse gives us two good reasons to praise God.

1. He is good
2. His mercy endureth forever

O give thanks unto the Lord; for He is good: because His mercy endureth for ever.

(Psalms 118:1 KJV)

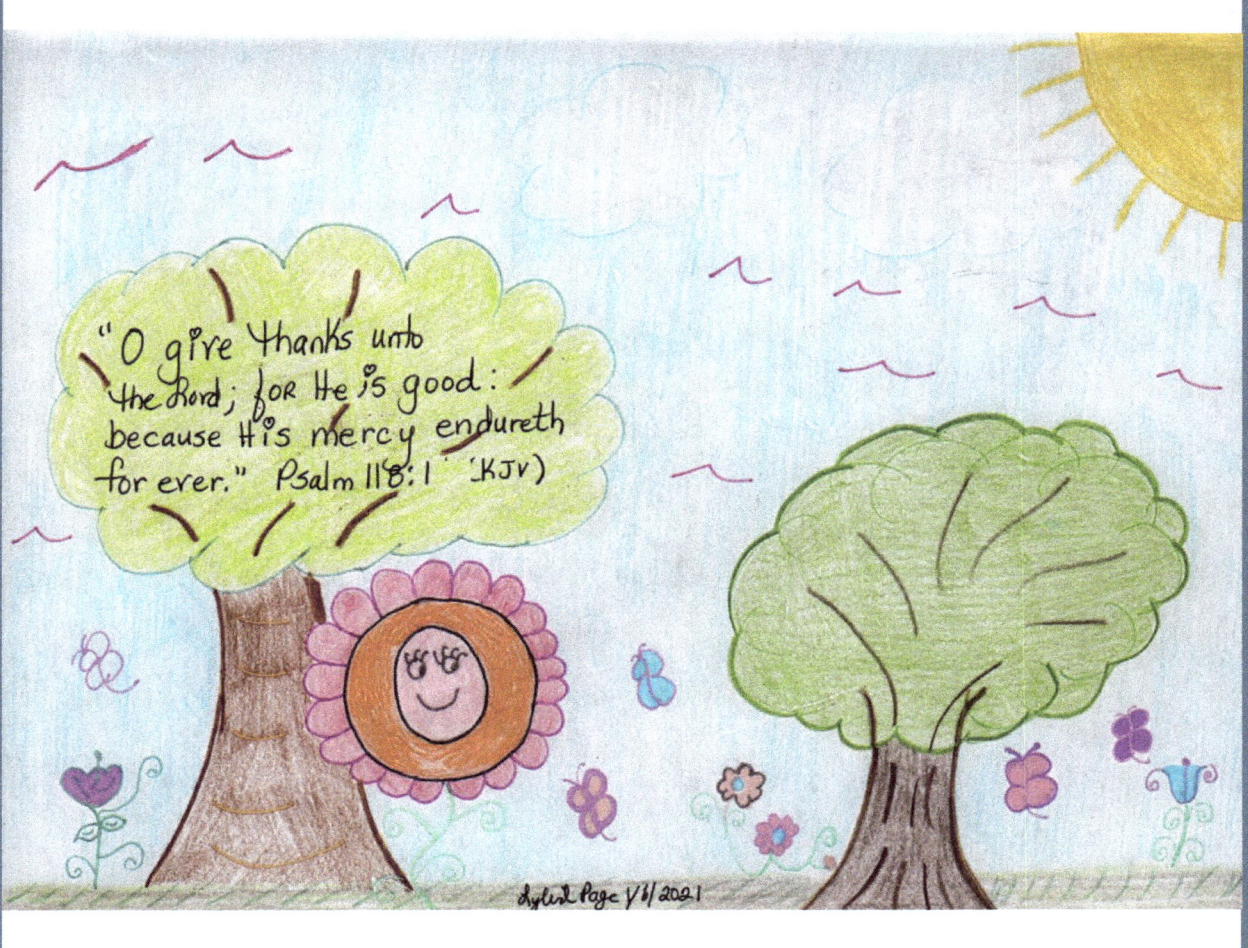

P

One sure way to stay focused as you walk daily with Christ is to spend time in prayer.

Pray without ceasing.

(1 Thessalonians 5:17 KJV)

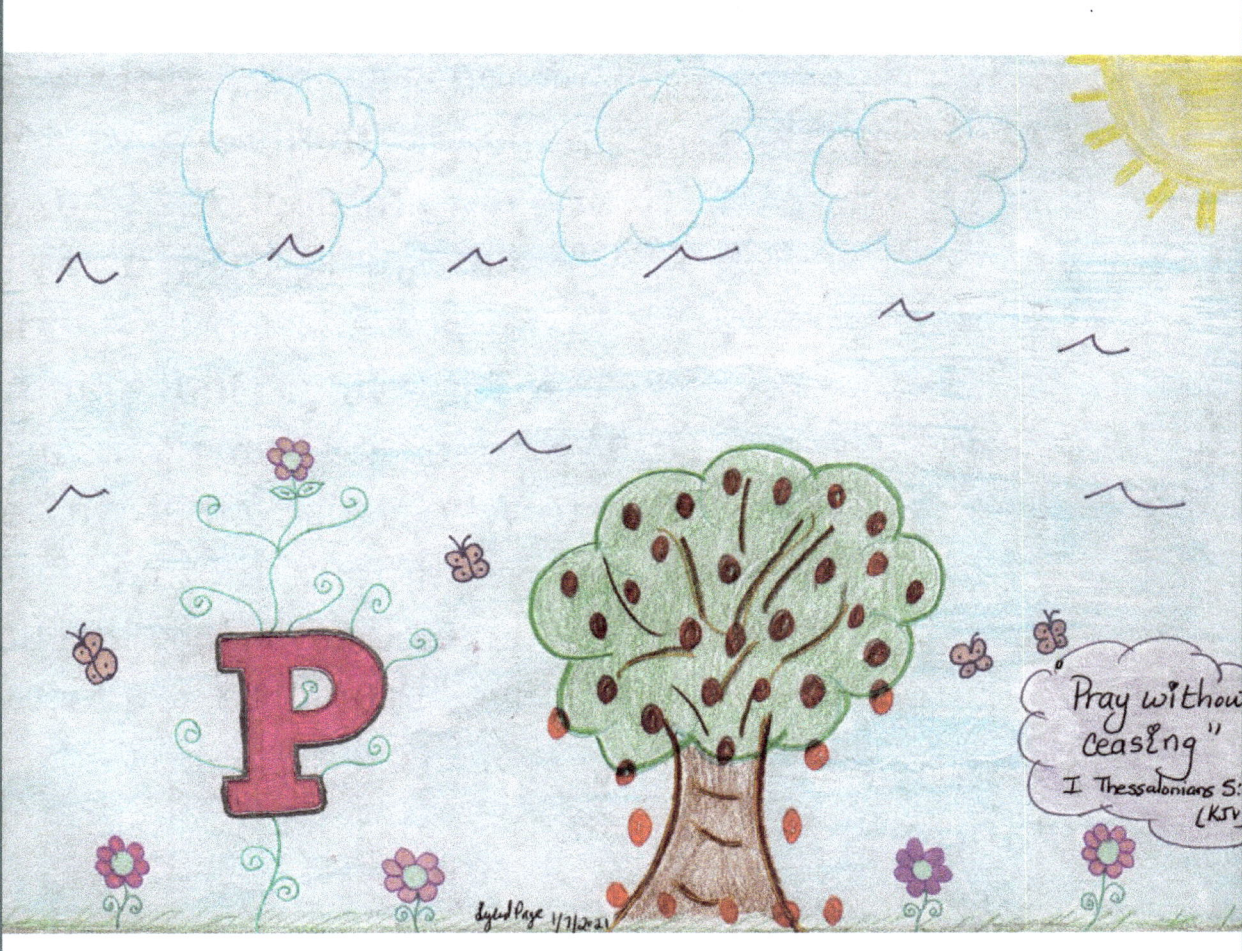

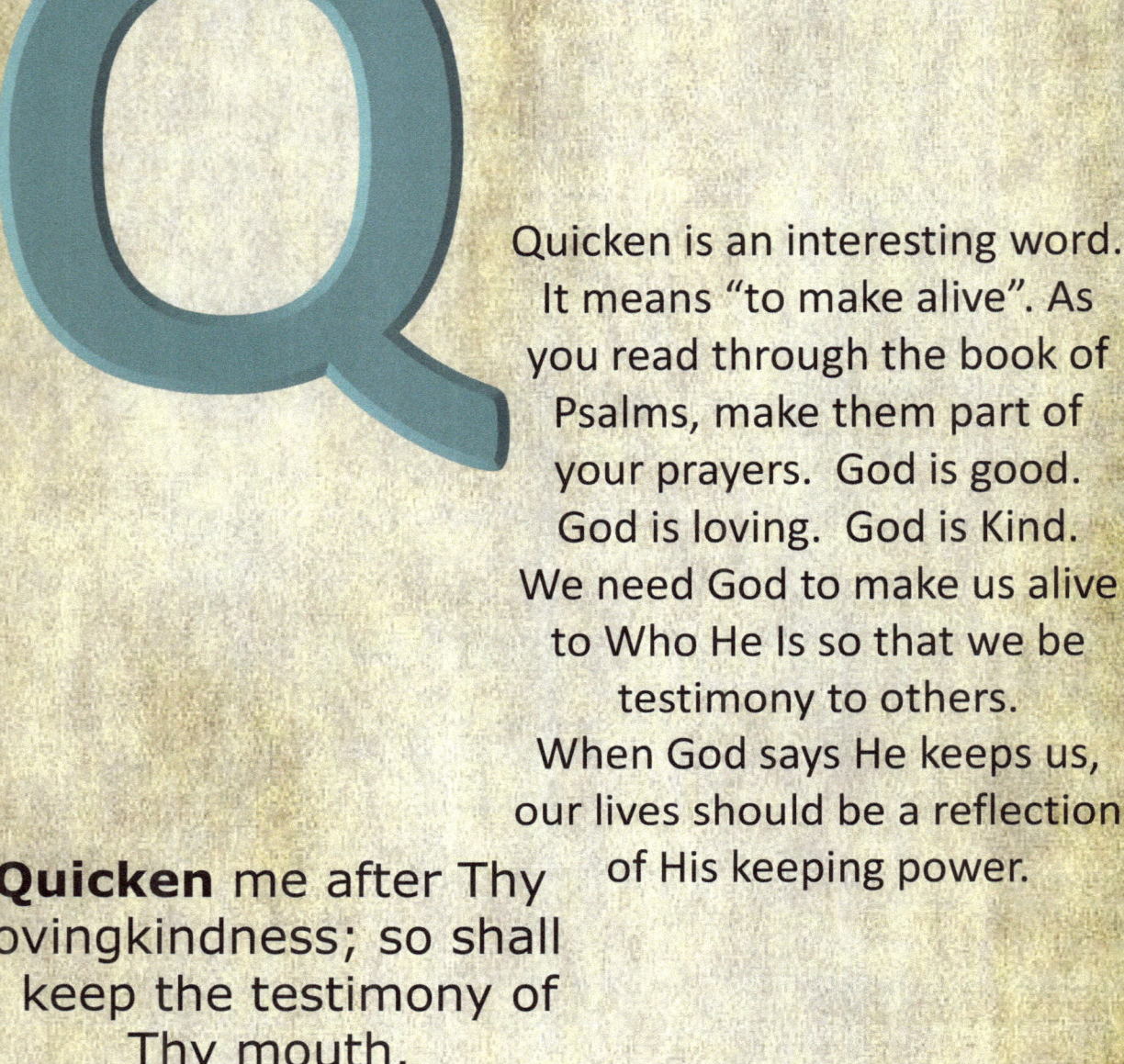

Quicken is an interesting word. It means "to make alive". As you read through the book of Psalms, make them part of your prayers. God is good. God is loving. God is Kind. We need God to make us alive to Who He Is so that we be testimony to others.
When God says He keeps us, our lives should be a reflection of His keeping power.

Quicken me after Thy lovingkindness; so shall I keep the testimony of Thy mouth.

(Psalms 119:88 KJV)

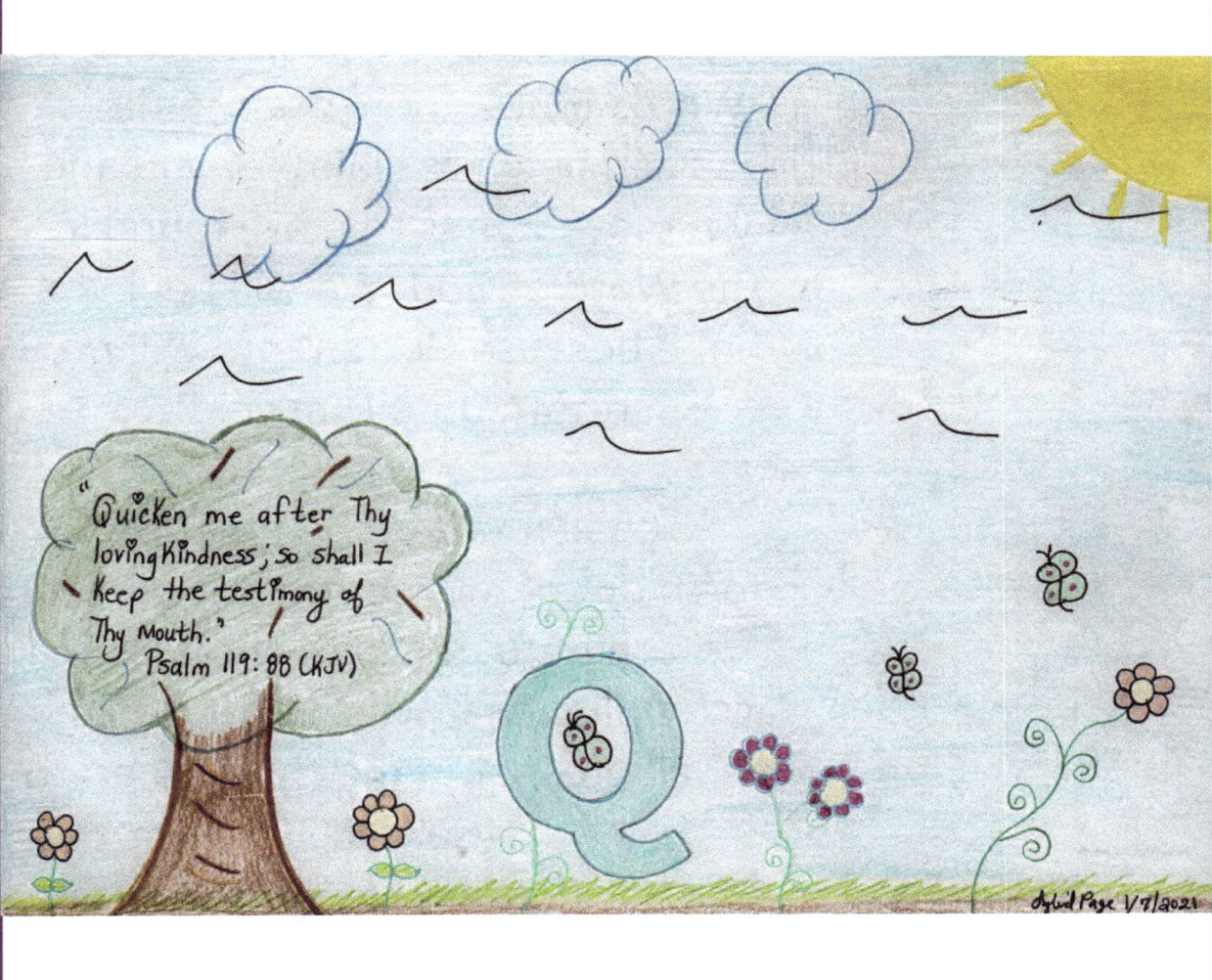

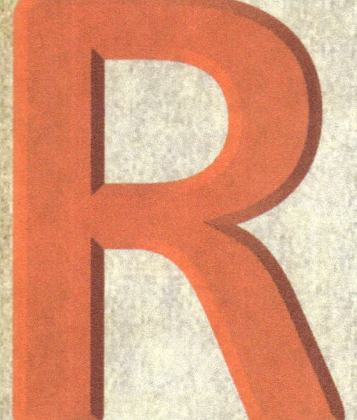

When life overwhelms us, we often time lose hope. It is during these times we need to remember what God has promised to us. Perhaps you have received a prophetic Word. If not, there are promises you can begin to claim for you and your loved ones that are found in the Word of God. We will begin to hope because God's Word will not return unto Him void.

"So shall my word be that goeth forth out of my mouth: it shall not return unto me void, but it shall accomplish that which I please, and it shall prosper in the thing whereto I sent it."
(Isaiah 55:11 KJV)

Remember the word unto Thy servant, upon which thou hast caused me to hope.

(Psalms 119:49 KJV)

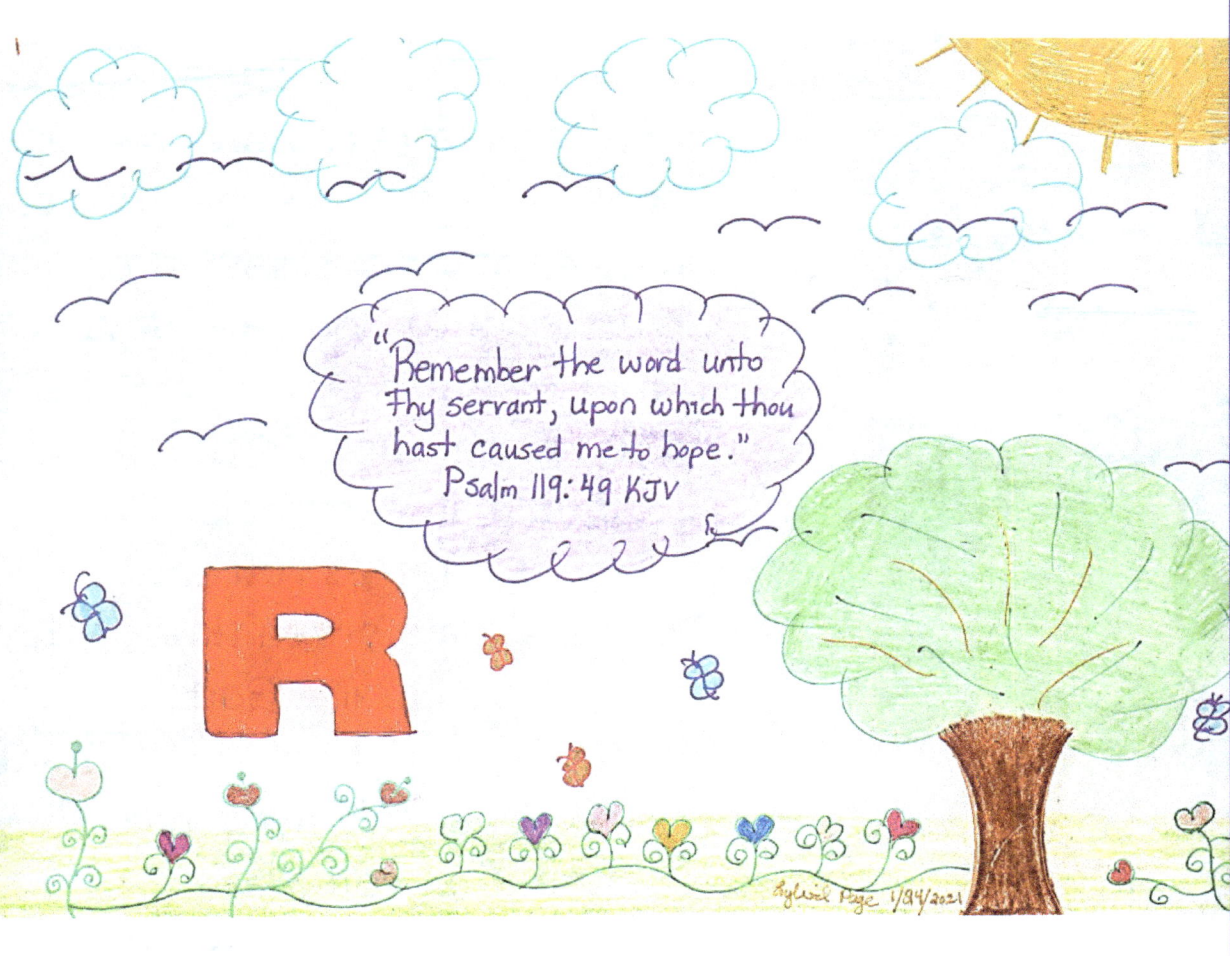

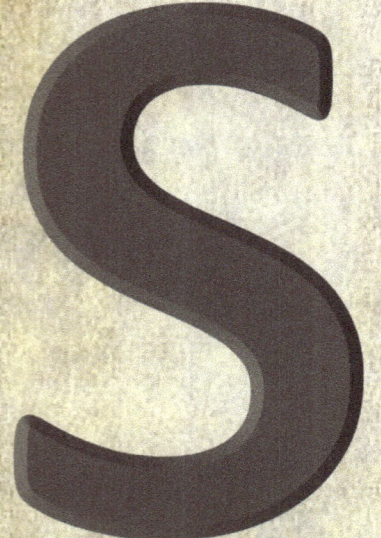

How many times do you
eat each day?
I am quite sure it is more than once.
For some it is more than twice.
So now I ask- how many times do
you praise God each day?
Is it just wants? Or is it not at all?
As you go throughout the day you
should at least praise God
as often as you eat.
This verse says seven times a day
do I praise God
because of His righteous judgments.
I challenge you to make
sure, that you praise God
at least seven times a day

Seven times a day do I praise Thee
because of Thy righteous judgments.

(Psalms 119:164 KJV)

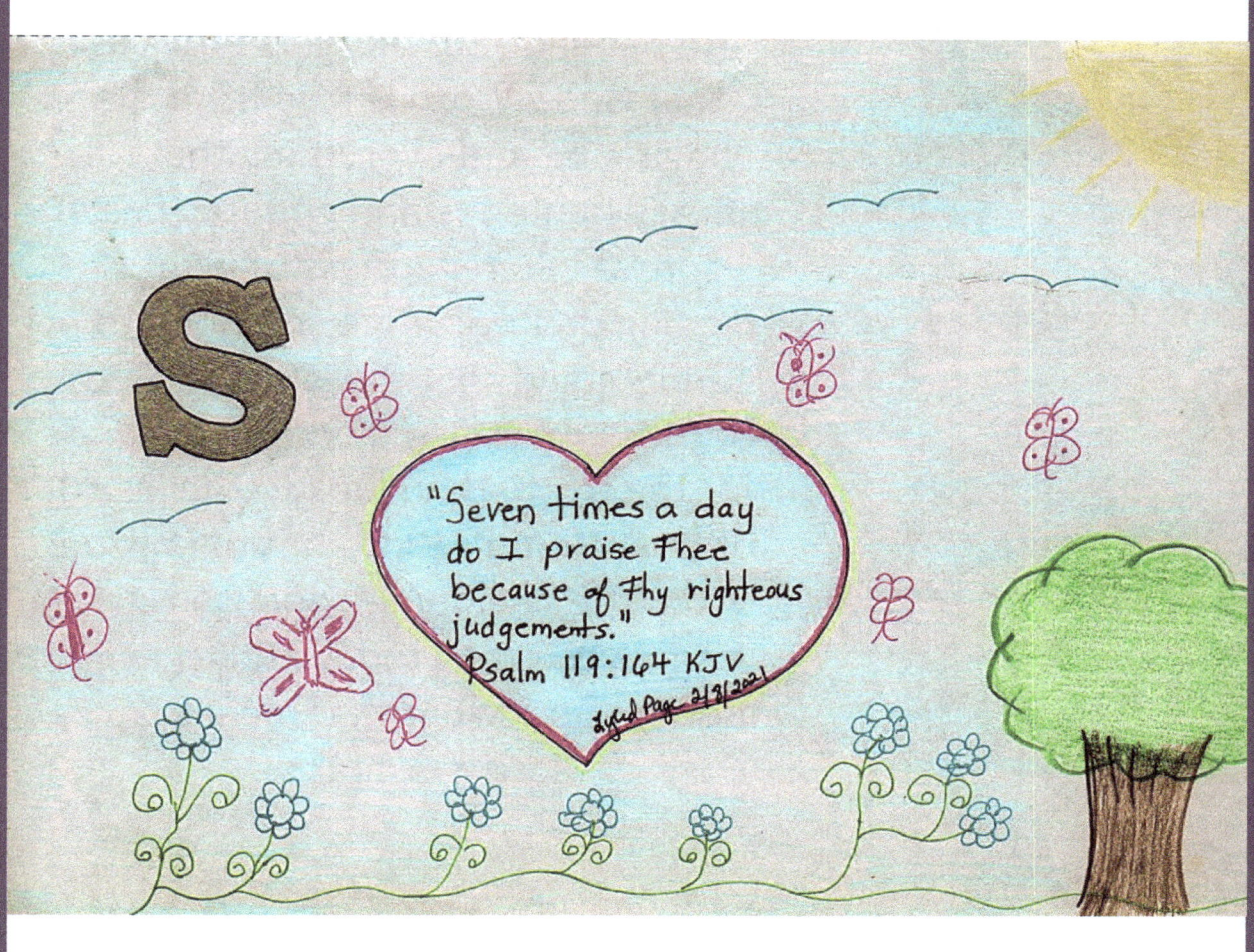

TAs a believer the most fundamental things for our lives is the Word of God. God does things based on what He has said. So, this verse tells us that God's Word is true from the beginning and everything that He does is righteous and endures (lasts) forever. So regardless of what is going on in your life you need to understand that the Word of God settles everything. If you're looking for the truth, then look to the Word of God. If God's Word has been true from the beginning - and He is the same yesterday today and forever more - guess what that means God's Word is true today.

Thy word is true from the beginning: and every one of Thy righteous judgments endureth for ever.

(Psalms 119:160 KJV)

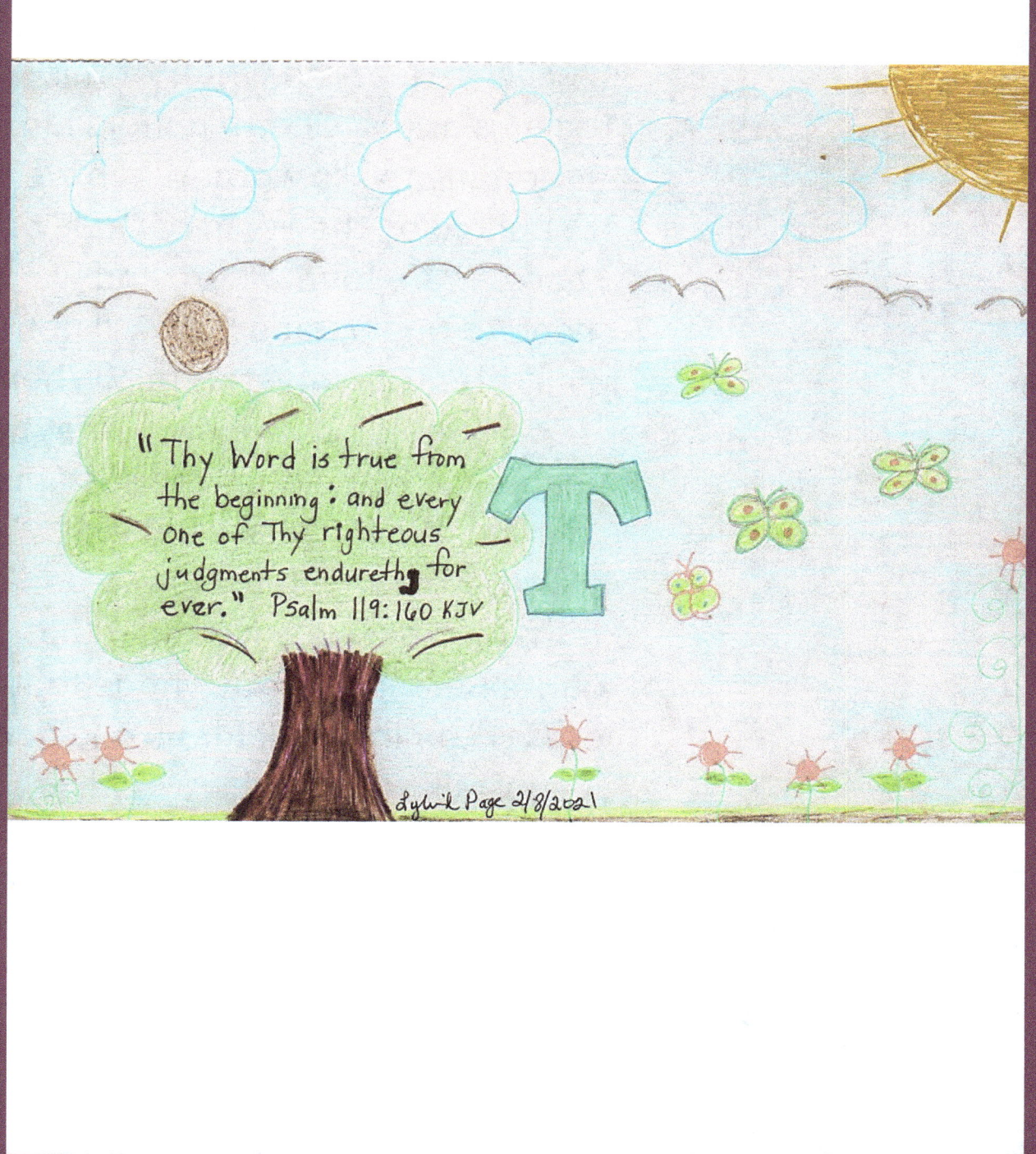

Now when we look at the word "uphold", we're looking at something that can carry our weight. Here the writer of this Psalm is asking God to uphold him according to His word. When we are upheld by the Word of God, we have a sure foundation, and we need to understand God will not fail us. He will not let us fall. When God upholds us, we live - that means God is the one who sustains our life. When we are upheld by God, we have no reason to be ashamed because we know that our hope is in God. Our hope that Jesus is coming back for us one day just like He said he would.

Uphold me according unto Thy Word, that I may live: and let me not be ashamed of my hope.

(Psalms 119:116 KJV)

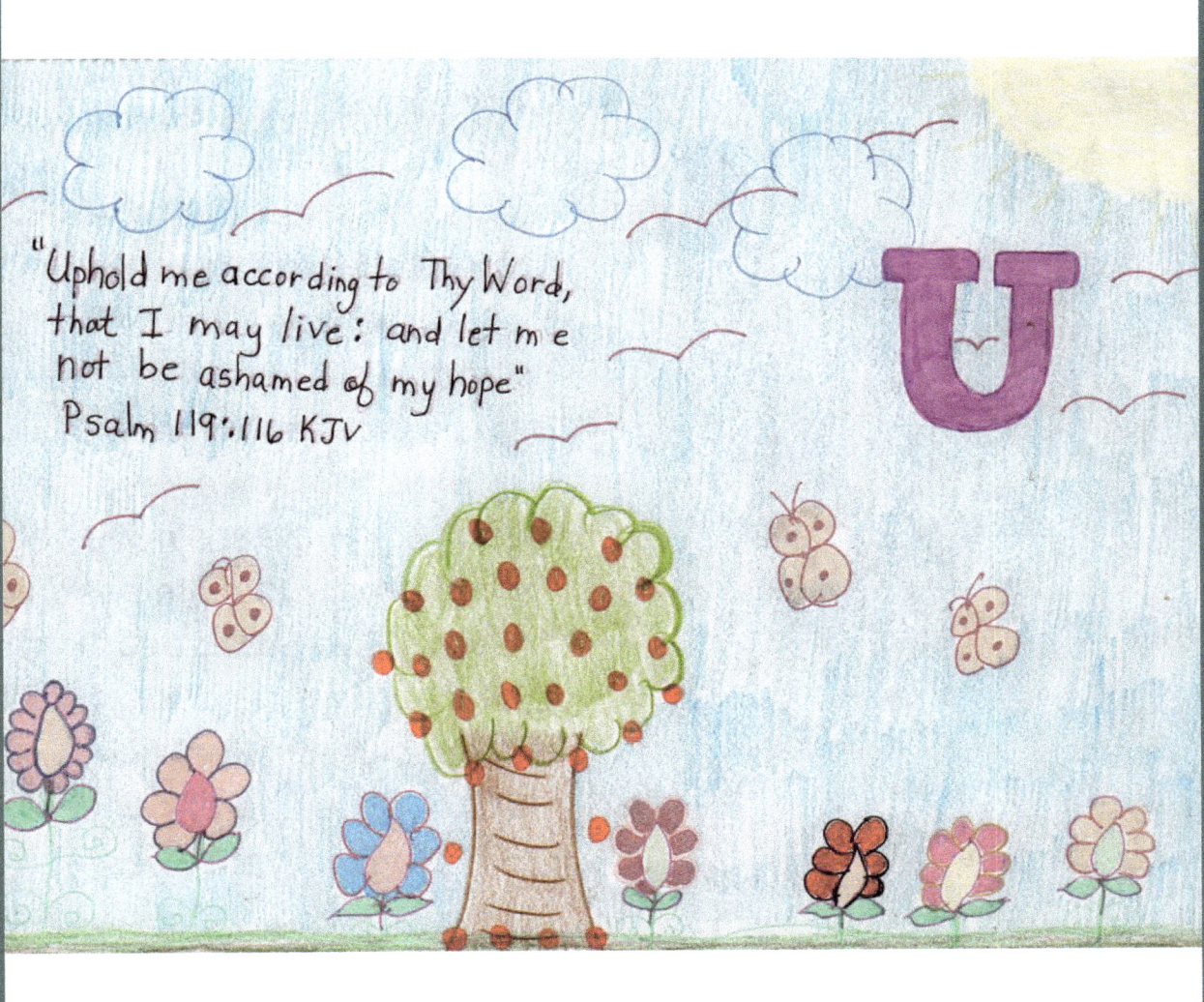

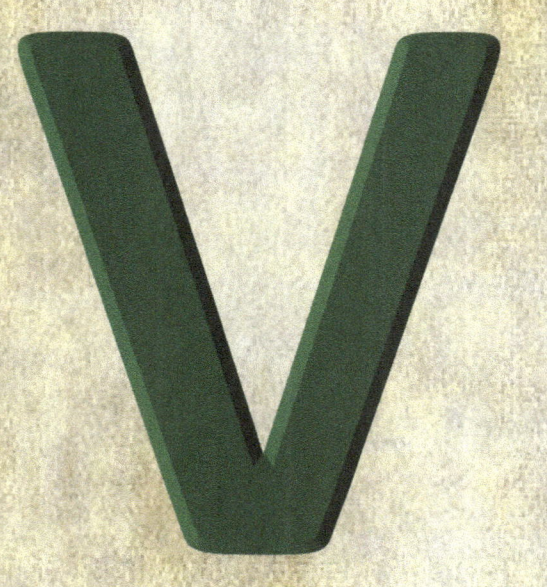

When something is repeated twice that is done for emphasis and it is done so that we will pay close attention to what's going to be said next. So, we look at the word "verily" in the scriptures it is saying - truly, this is a fact. So, Jesus is saying into us that if we keep His saying that means if we pay attention to what He has said we will never see death. In other words when this physical existence that we're in is over - that's not the end of our story – the best is yet to come.

Verily, verily, I say unto you,
If a man keep My saying,
he shall never see death.

(John 8:51 KJV)

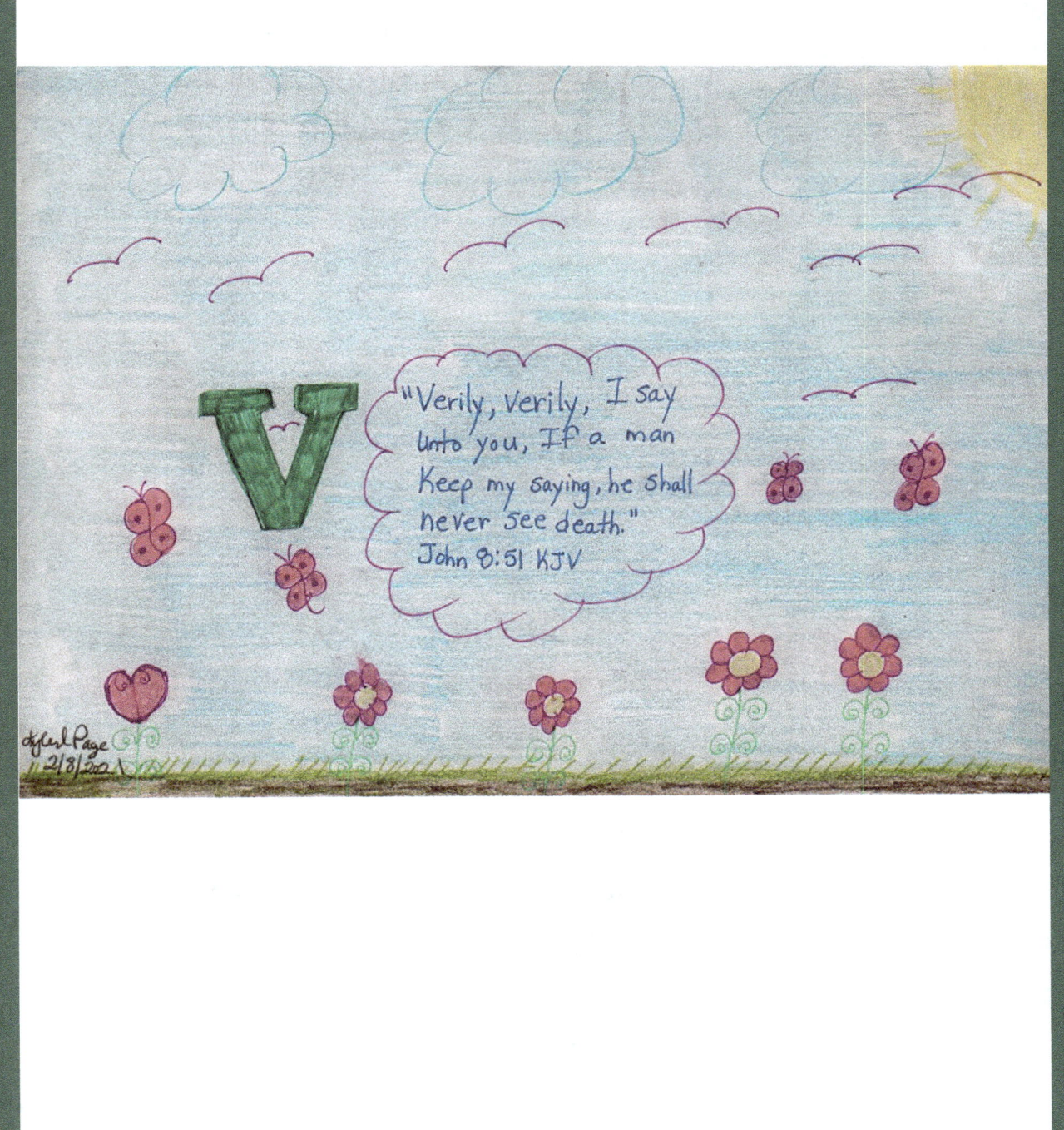

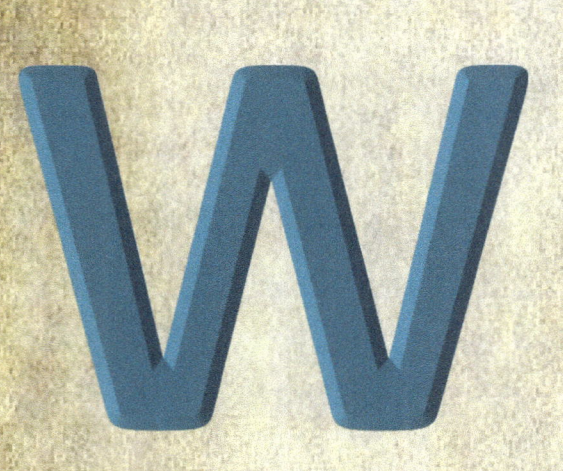

How many of us like waiting? Not many for sure. We live in a microwave society where we want things, and we want them now. When we get to a red light, we want it to immediately turn green. But here the Bible tells us that we need to wait on the Lord.
Why wait on the Lord? As believers we are to be following God.
You can not follow if you are trying to lead the way.

Our part:
1. Wait on the Lord
2. Be of good courage

God's part:
He shall strengthen thine heart

Wait on the LORD: be of good courage, and He shall strengthen thine heart: wait, I say, on the LORD.

(Psalms 27:14 KJV)

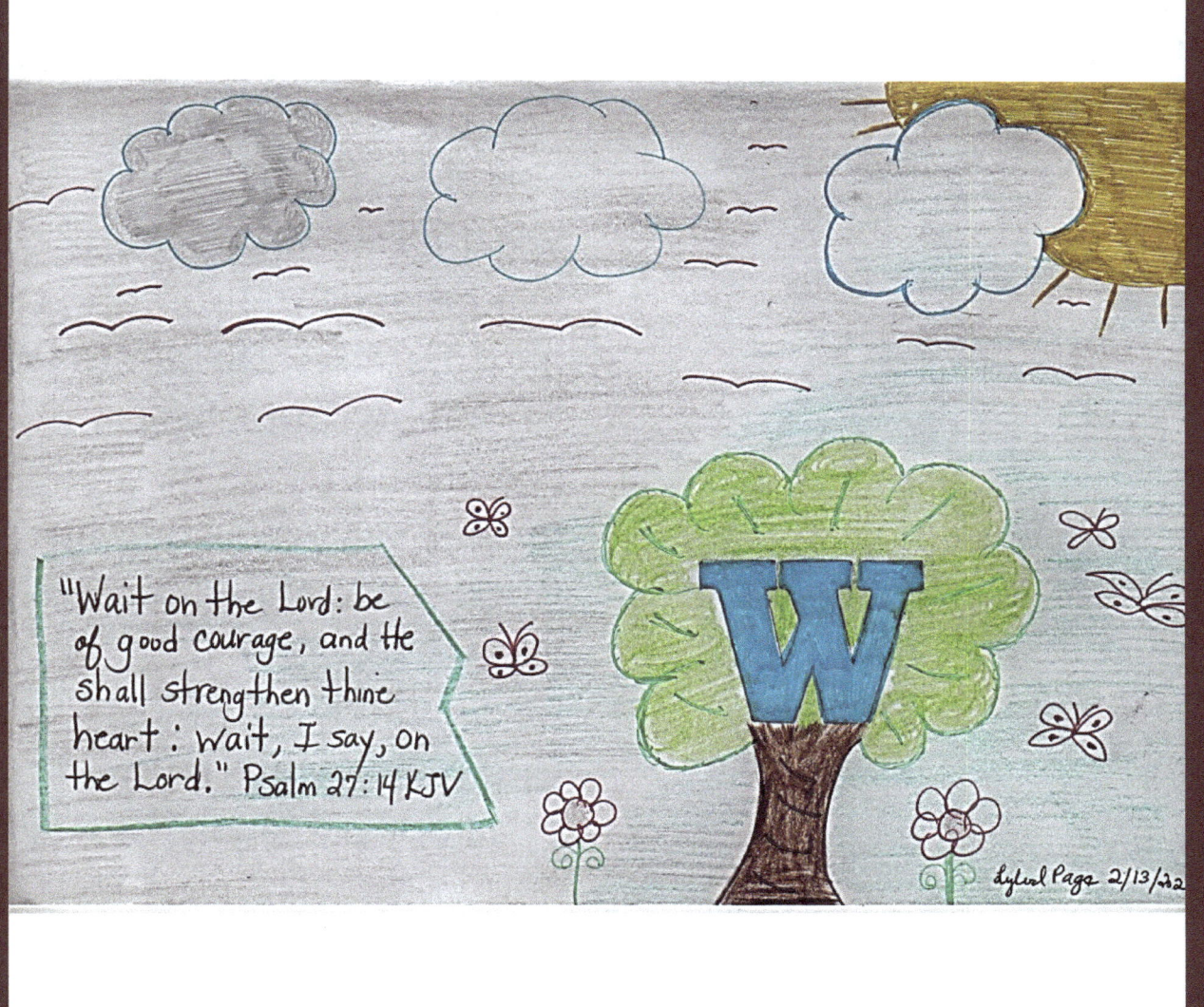

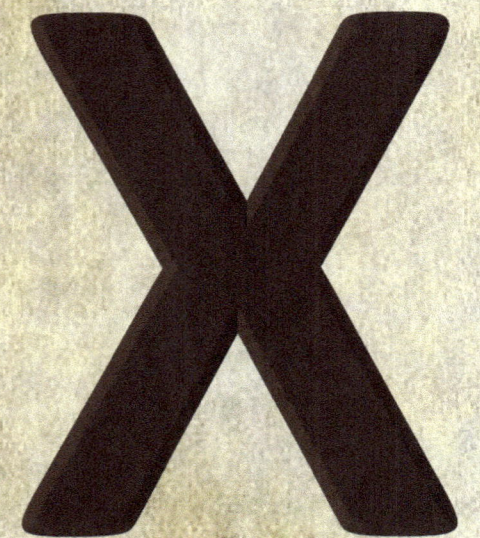

Do you like it when you receive an award? Do you like to be celebrated? When was the last time you celebrated God?
We are to exalt the Lord. Exalt means to promote, to lift, to praise. We are to lift God above ourselves and the problems we may be facing. We are also to lift God up above our successes. We are to worship
God each day. The Lord our God is Holy and He is worthy of all our praise all the days of our lives.

EXalt the LORD our God,
and worship at his holy hill;
for the LORD our God is holy.

(Psalms 99:9 KJV)

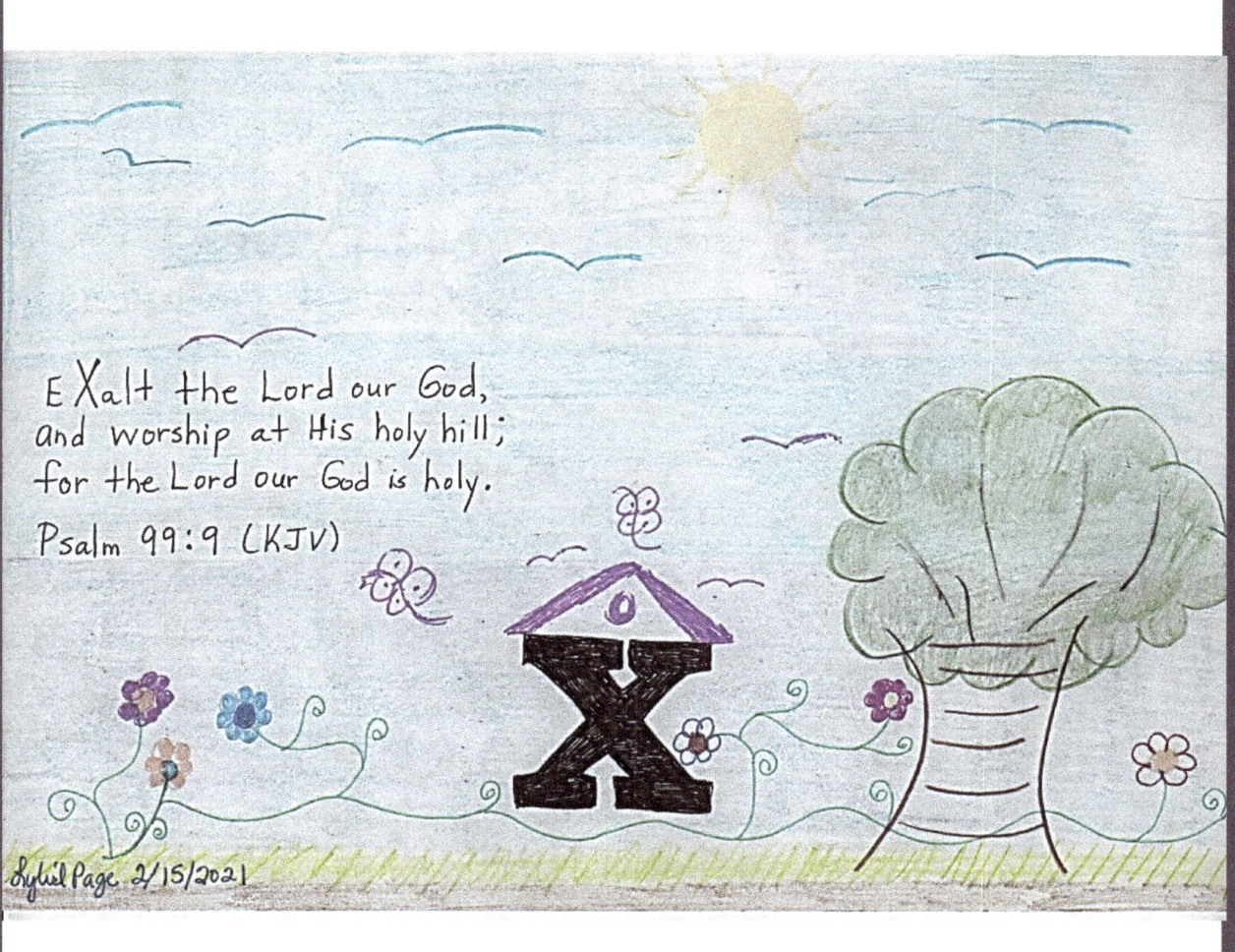

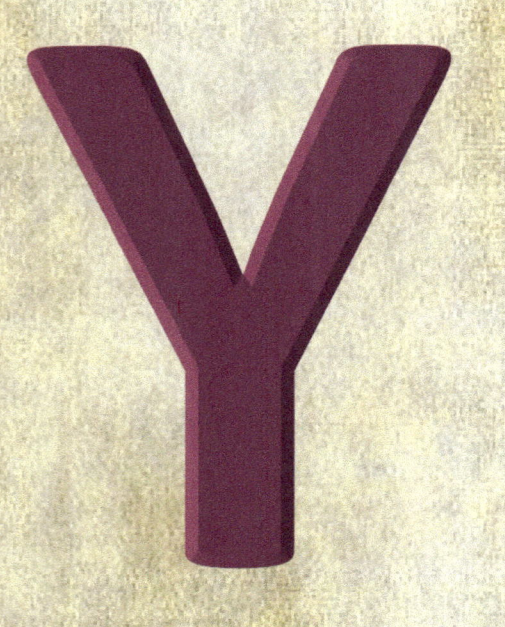

"The earth is the Lord's, and the fulness thereof; the world, and they that dwell therein. "
(Psalms 24:1 KJV)

"Ye" is the person who is reading this right now. Yes, that means you and it means me. It is one thing to be blessed by people, but you know you are blessed when you are blessed by the Lord – the Maker of Heaven and Earth.

Ye are blessed of the LORD which made heaven and earth.

(Psalms 115:15 KJV)

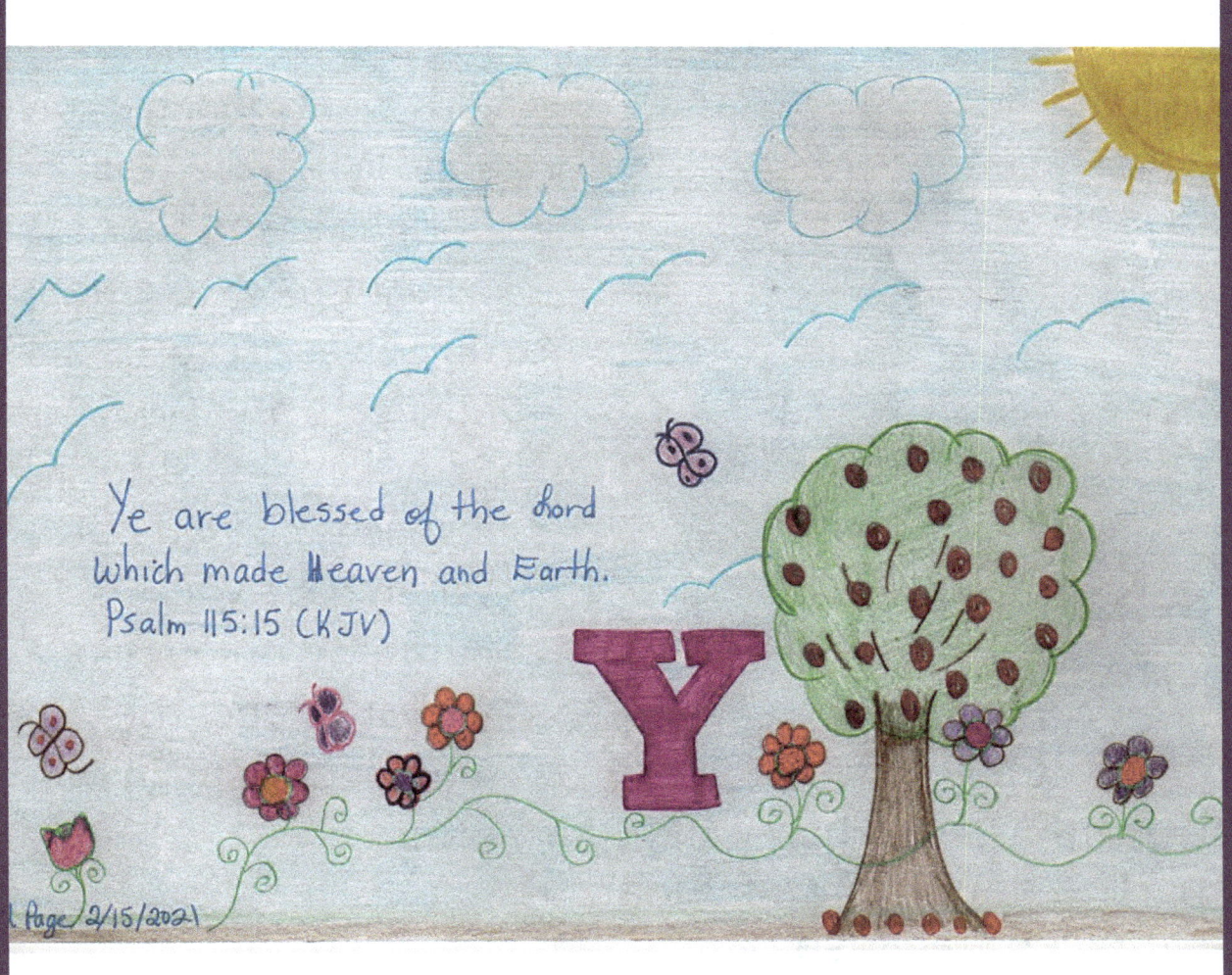

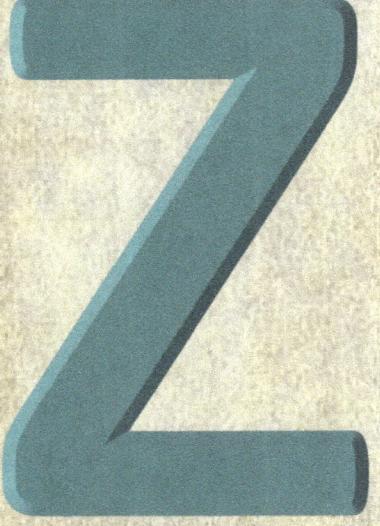

Most of us think of judgments in a negative way. When we walk upright - God sees. We will not have to defend ourselves. Jesus is our advocate and God, our Father, makes sure His justice is carried out. When have walked humbly with our God, we can expect the judgment to be in our favor.

Zion heard, and was glad; and the daughters of Judah rejoiced because of Thy judgments, O Lord.

(Psalms 97:8 KJV)

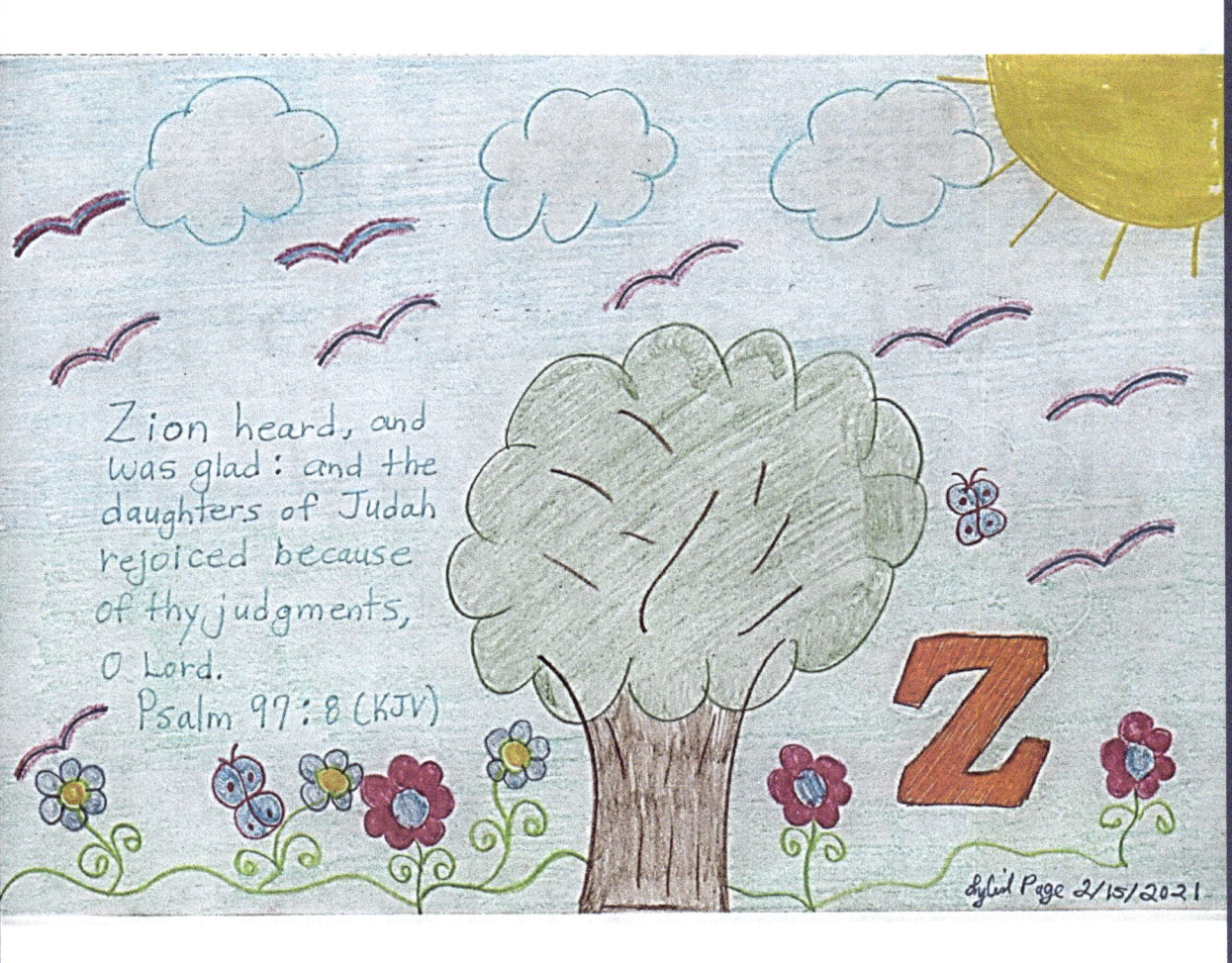

Thy word have I hid in mine heart, that I might not sin against Thee.

(Psalms 119:11 KJV)

Scripture References

Ask – Matthew 7:7
Blessed – Psalm 1:1
Come – Matthew 11:28
Delight – Psalm 37:4
Enter – Psalm 100:4
For – Psalm 100:5
Give – Luke 6:38
Hold – Psalm 17:5
I – Psalm 3:5
Judge – Matthew 7:1
Keep – Proverbs 4:23
Let – Psalm 19:14
Make – Psalm 100:1
Not – Psalm 115:1
O - Psalm 118:1
Pray - 1 Thessalonians 5:17
Quicken – Psalm 119:88
Remember - Psalm 119:49
Seven – Psalm 119:164
Thy – Psalm 119:160
Uphold – Psalm 119:116
Verily – John 8:51
Wait – Psalm 27:14
e**X**alt – Psalm 99:9
Ye – Psalm 115:15
Zion – Psalm 97:8

I pray you have ben encouraged and inspired.
Share this book with your family and friends.

The LORD bless thee, and keep thee:
The LORD make His face shine upon thee,
and be gracious unto thee:
The LORD lift up His countenance upon thee,
and give thee peace.
(Numbers 6:24-26 KJV)

The proceeds from this book will be used to help support the

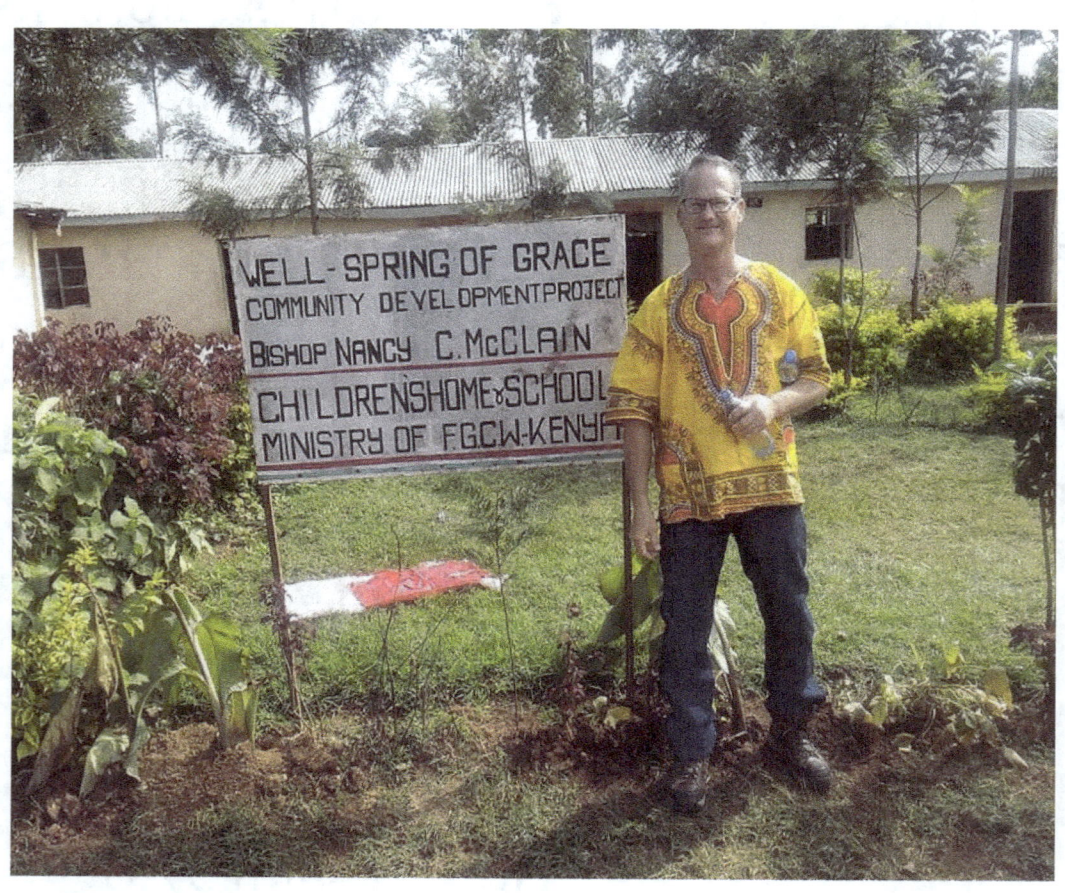

About the author

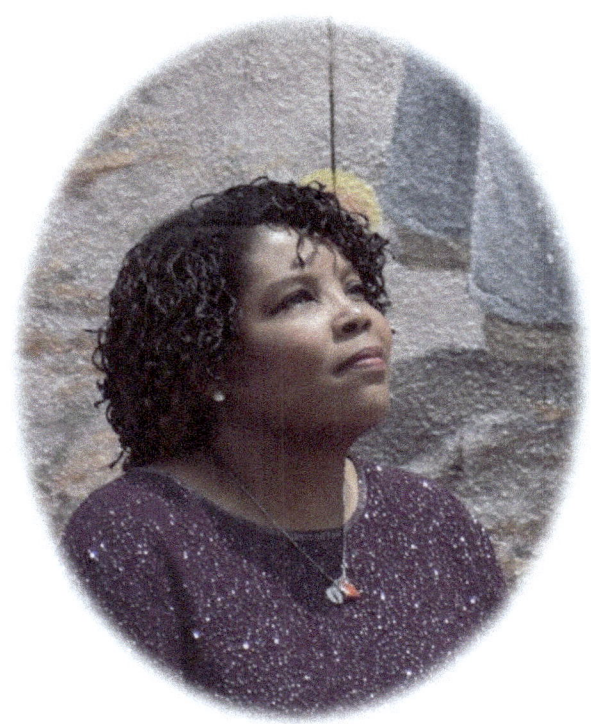

Lybid gave her life to Christ at an early age. Writing is something she has always enjoyed doing from before she started school. She is creative. She writes, draws, and sometimes even paints. She is actively involved in the churches she attends. She preaches, teaches, and leads worship. She is also the author of "Prayer Is..." which is also available on Amazon.

She has been married to Timothy Page, Sr. for 21 plus years. They have five wonderful children - James, Deborah, Elijah, Timothy Jr., Elizabeth; one great daughter in-law – Amber; seven awesome grandchildren -Hannah, Ezzrah, Erik, Elisha, sunset, Merickah, Mordarkye. Lybid looks forward to seeing the goodness of God touch the life of each person she meets.

Lybid Page was born November 23, 1970, to Deaureal and Vertis Bell in Atlanta, Georgia. She is the oldest of four daughters. She currently resides in Lindsay CA with her husband and their four youngest children.

ABCDEFG
HIJKLMNO
PQRSTUV
WXYZ!?.,

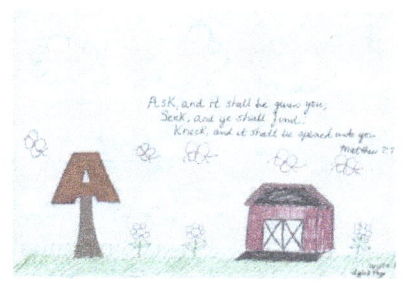 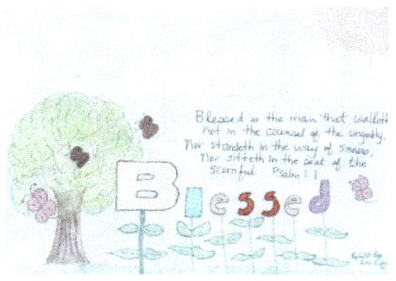 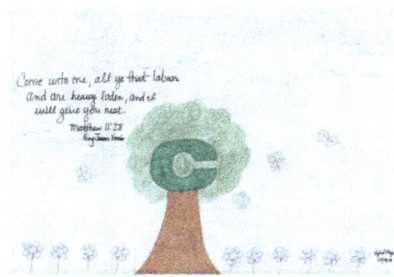
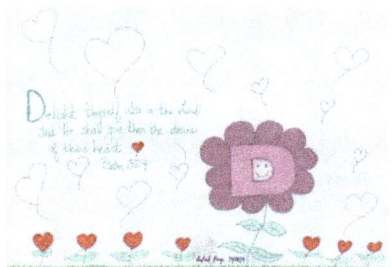 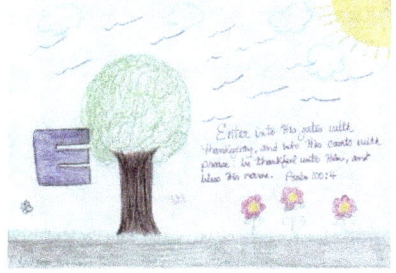 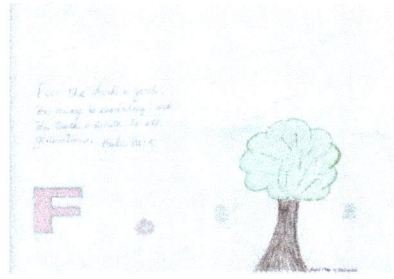
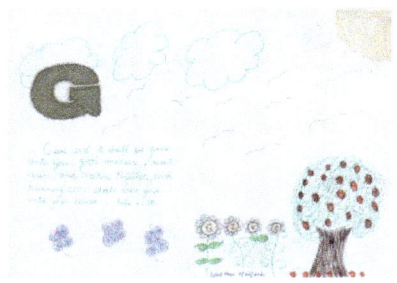 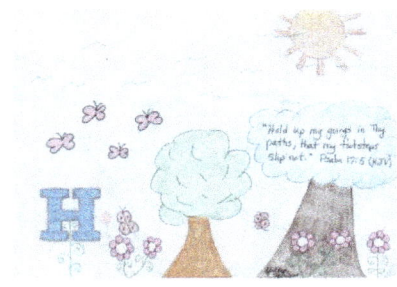 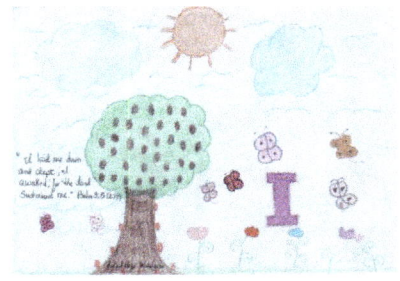
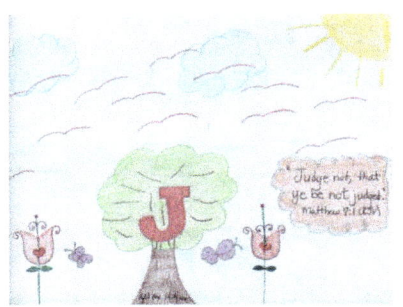 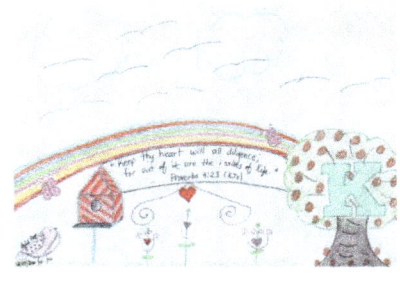 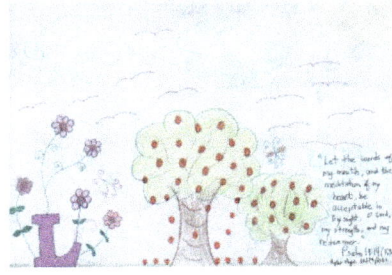
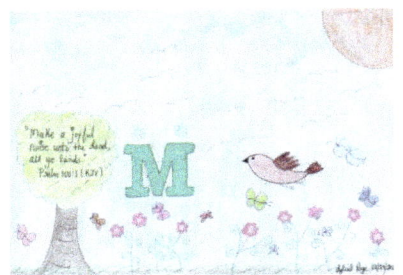 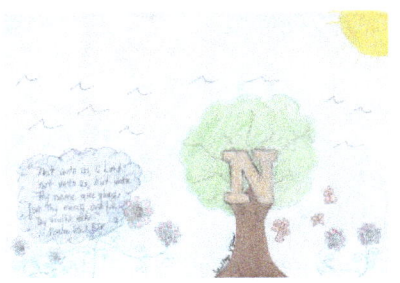 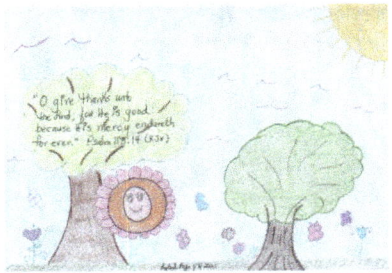

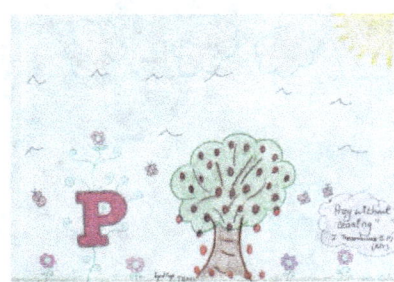
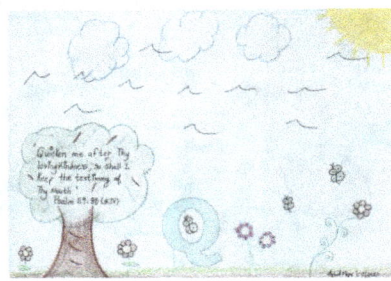
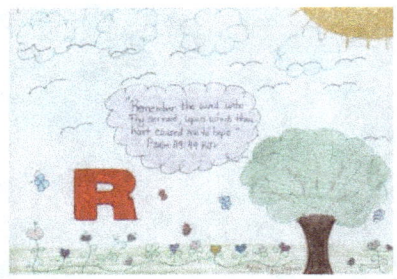
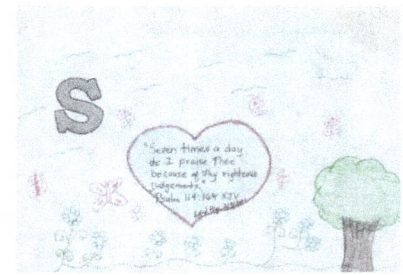
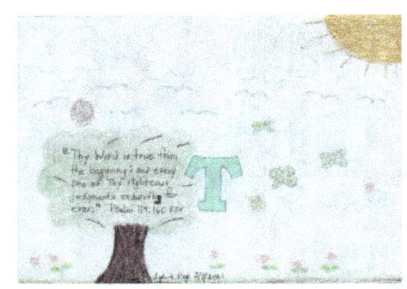
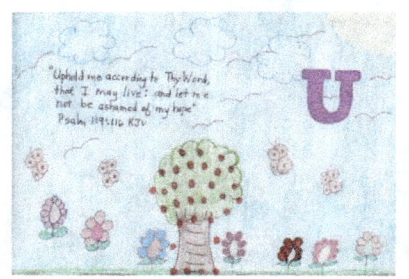
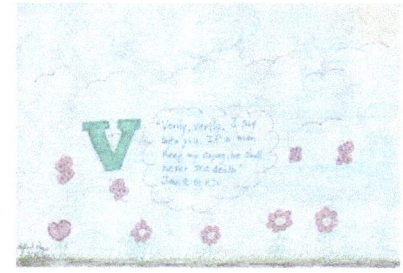
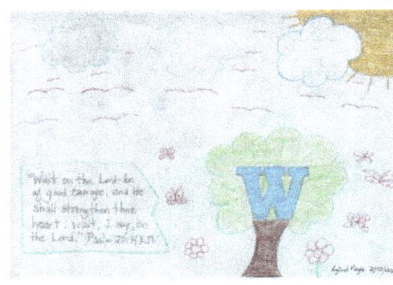
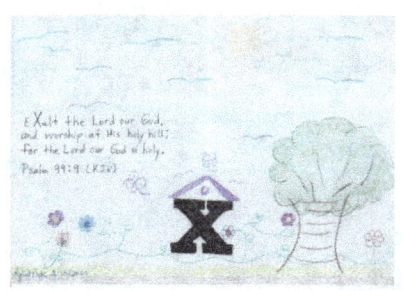
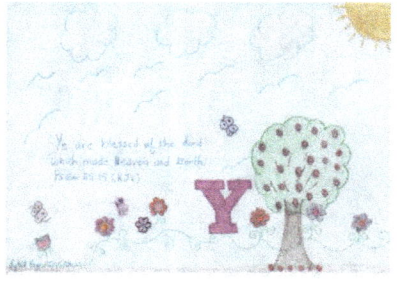
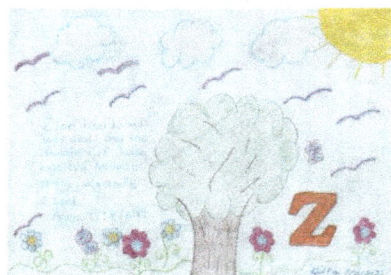

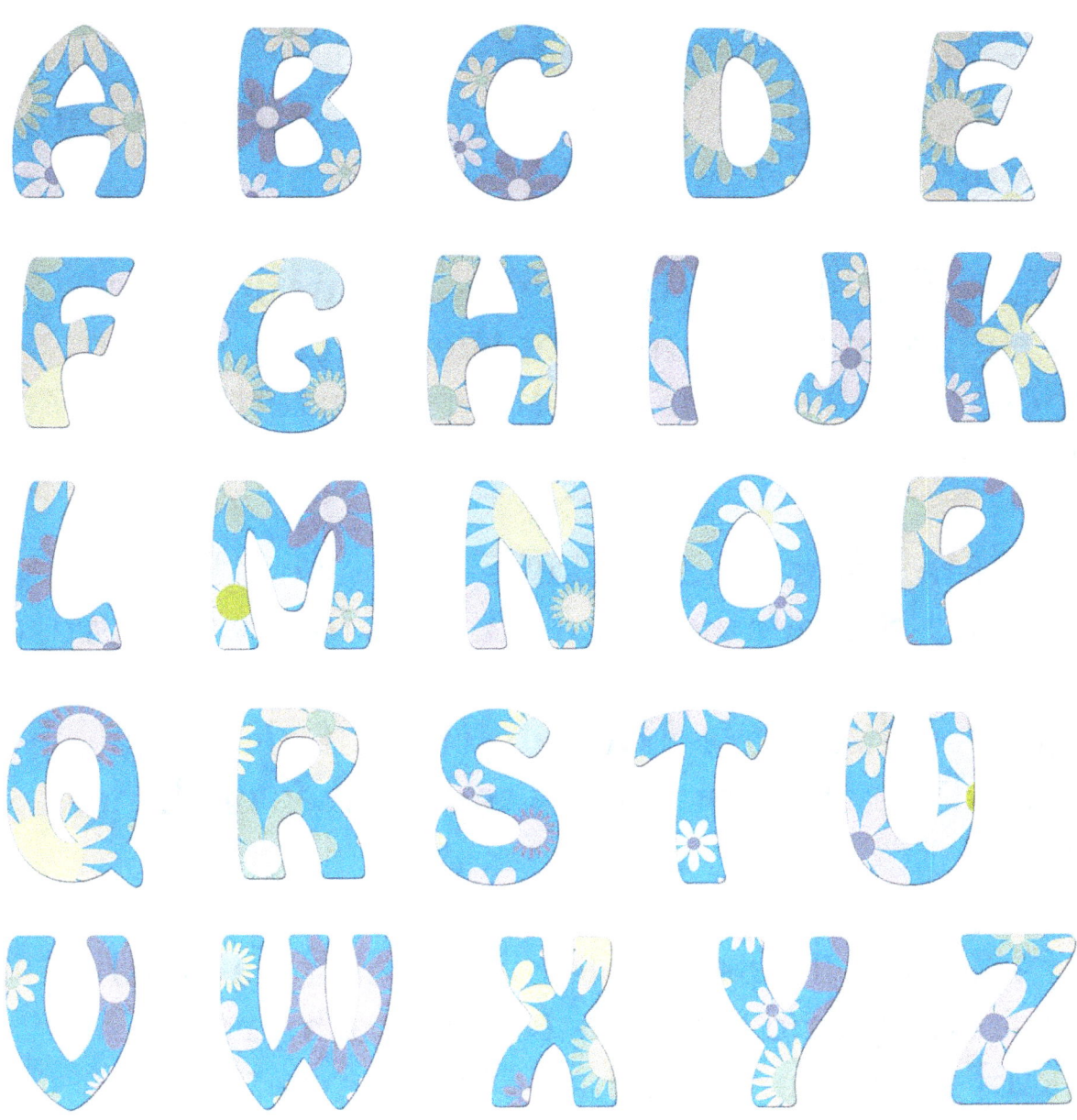

Scriptures

Ask – Matthew 7:7 - Ask, and it shall be given you; seek, and ye shall find; knock, and it shall be opened unto you:

Blessed – Psalm 1:1 - Blessed is the man that walketh not in the counsel of the ungodly, nor standeth in the way of sinners, nor sitteth in the seat of the scornful.

Come – Matthew 11:28 - Come unto Me, all ye that labour and are heavy laden, and I will give you rest.

Delight – Psalm 37:4 - Delight thyself also in the Lord; and He shall give thee the desires of thine heart.

Enter – Psalm 100:4 - Enter into His gates with thanksgiving, and into His courts with praise: be thankful unto Him, and bless His Name.

Scriptures

For – Psalm 100:5 - For the Lord is good; His mercy is everlasting; and His truth endureth to all generations.

Give – Luke 6:38 - Give, and it shall be given unto you; good measure, pressed down, and shaken together, and running over, shall men give into your bosom. For with the same measure that ye mete withal it shall be measured to you again.

Hold – Psalm 17:5 - Hold up my goings in thy paths, that my footsteps slip not.

I – Psalm 3:5 - I laid me down and slept; I awaked; for the Lord sustained me.

Judge – Matthew 7:1 - Judge not, that ye be not judged.

Scriptures

Keep – Proverbs 4:23 - Keep thy heart with all diligence; for out of it are the issues of life.

Let – Psalm 19:14 - Let the words of my mouth, and the meditation of my heart, be acceptable in Thy sight, O Lord, my Strength, and my Redeemer.

Make – Psalm 100:1 - A Psalm of praise. Make a joyful noise unto the Lord, all ye lands.

Not – Psalm 115:1 - Not unto us, O Lord, not unto us, but unto Thy name give glory, for Thy mercy, and for Thy truth's sake.

O - Psalm 118:1 - O give thanks unto the Lord; for He is good: because His mercy endureth for ever.

Scriptures

Pray - 1 Thessalonians 5:17 - Pray without ceasing.

Quicken – Psalm 119:88 - Quicken me after Thy lovingkindness; so shall I keep the testimony of Thy mouth.

Remember - Psalm 119:49 - Hear my voice according unto Thy lovingkindness: O Lord, quicken me according to Thy judgment.

Seven – Psalm 119:164 - Seven times a day do I praise thee because of Thy righteous judgments.

Thy – Psalm 119:160 - Thy word is true from the beginning: and every one of Thy righteous judgments endureth for ever.

Scriptures

Uphold – Psalm 119:116 - Uphold me according unto Thy Word, that I may live: and let me not be ashamed of my hope.

Verily – John 8:51 - Verily, verily, I say unto you, If a man keep My saying, he shall never see death.

Wait – Psalm 27:14 - Wait on the Lord: be of good courage, and He shall strengthen thine heart: wait, I say, on the Lord.

e**X**alt – Psalm 99:9 - Exalt the Lord our God, and worship at His holy hill; for the Lord our God is holy.

Ye – Psalm 115:15 - Ye are blessed of the Lord which made heaven and earth.

Zion – Psalm 97:8 "Zion heard, and was glad; and the daughters of Judah rejoiced because of Thy judgments, O Lord."

www.ingramcontent.com/pod-product-compliance
Lightning Source LLC
Chambersburg PA
CBHW080618220526
45466CB00010B/3376